Critical Thinking
and
Ethics

PHI 2604

Melissa Lammey

Change the course.

Acknowledgments:

pp. 2–25, 28–48: From *Critical Thinking: A Student's Introduction*, 5th edition, by Gregory Bassham, William Irwin, Henry Nardone, and James Wallace. Copyright © 2013. Published by McGraw-Hill, Inc.

pp. 49–59: From *Thinking Critically,* 9th edition, by John Chaffe. Copyright © 2009 by Cengage Learning, Inc. Reprinted by permission of the publisher via the Copyright Clearance Center.

pp. 62–90: From *An Introduction to Logic* by Kurt Mosser. Copyright © 2011. Published by Bridgepoint Education. Reprinted by permission.

pp. 92–111, 115, 117, 123, 134, 136, 140, 142, 145, 148, 150, 152, 153, 155, 157, 159, 161, 162: From *The Power of Critical Thinking* by Lewis Vaughn. Copyright © 2013 by Oxford University Press, NY. Reprinted by permission of the publisher via the Copyright Clearance Center.

pp. 114–115: As appeared on *USA Today* online, April 28, 2003. Copyright © 2003 by Gannett Co., Inc. Reprinted by permission of the publisher via the Copyright Clearance Center.

pp. 116–117: From ESL Planet by Bill Daly. Copyright © 2003 by Bill Daly. Reprinted by permission of the author.

pp. 118–123: As appeared in *Free Inquiry*, Vol. 17, No. 4, 1997. Copyright © 1997 by The Council for Secular Humanism. Reprinted by permission.

pp. 124–134: From *Debating the Ethics, Science, and Culture of Homosexuality* by John Corvino. Copyright © 1997 by Rowman & Littlefield Publishers, Inc. Reprinted by permission of the publisher via the Copyright Clearance Center.

pp. 135–136: As appeared on TownHall.com, June 17, 2003. Copyright © 2003 by TownHall.com.

pp. 137–140: As appeared in *QQ: Report from the Center for Philosophy and Public Policy*, Vol. 6, No. 1, Winter, 1986. Copyright © 1986 by the Institute for Philosophy and Public Policy.

pp. 141–142: As appeared in the *Buffalo Evening News*, December 5, 2010. Copyright © 2010 by Caroline Baum. Reprinted by permission of the publisher via the Copyright Clearance Center.

pp. 143–145: As appeared in *Focus on the Family*, June/July, 2003. Copyright © 2003 by Neil Clark Warren.

pp. 146–147: As appeared in the *Los Angeles Times*, July 18, 2011. Copyright © 2011 by the Los Angeles Times Syndicate. Reprinted by permission of the publisher via the Copyright Clearance Center.

pp. 149–150: As appeared in the *Los Angeles Times*, January 13, 2011. Copyright © 2011 by the Los Angeles Times Syndicate. Reprinted by permission of the publisher via the Copyright Clearance Center.

Change the course.

530 Great Road
Acton, MA 01720
800-562-2147

Contents

1

Chapter 1: What Is Critical Thinking?

What Is Critical Thinking?

Gregory Bassham et al

> The function of education is to teach one to think intensively and to think critically.
>
> —Martin Luther King Jr.

Often when we use the word *critical* we mean "negative and fault-finding." This is the sense we have in mind, for example, when we complain about a parent or a friend who we think is unfairly critical of what we do or say. But *critical* also means "involving or exercising skilled judgment or observation." In this sense critical thinking means thinking clearly and intelligently More precisely, **critical thinking** is the general term given to a wide range of cognitive skills and intellectual dispositions needed to effectively identify, analyze, and evaluate arguments and truth claims; to discover and overcome personal preconceptions and biases; to formulate and present convincing reasons in support of conclusions; and to make reasonable, intelligent decisions about what to believe and what to do.

Put somewhat differently, critical thinking is disciplined thinking governed by clear intellectual standards. Among the most important of these intellectual standards are **clarity, precision, accuracy, relevance, consistency, logical correctness, completeness**, and **fairness**. Let's begin our introduction to critical thinking by looking briefly at each of these important critical thinking standards.

> The purpose which runs through all other educational purposes—the common thread of education—is the development of the ability to think.
>
> —Educational Policies Commission

Critical Thinking Standards

Clarity

Before we can effectively evaluate a person's argument or claim, we need to understand clearly what he or she is saying. Unfortunately, that can be difficult because people often fail to express themselves clearly. Sometimes this lack of clarity is due to laziness, carelessness, or a lack of skill. At other times it results from a misguided effort to appear clever, learned, or profound. Consider the following passage from philosopher Martin Heidegger's influential but notoriously obscure book *Being and Time*:

> Everything that can be said can be said clearly.
>
> —Ludwig Wittgenstein

Temporality makes possible the unity of existence, facticity, and falling, and in this way constitutes primordially the totality of the structure of care. The items of care have not been pieced together cumulatively any more than temporality itself has been put together "in the course of time" ["mit der Zeit"] out of the future, the having been, and the Present. Temporality "is" not an entity at all. It is not, but it temporalizes itself. . . .Temporality temporalizes, and indeed it temporalizes possible ways of itself. These make possible the multiplicity of Dasein's modes of Being, and especially the basic possibility of authentic or inauthentic existence.

That may be profound, or it may be nonsense, or it may be both. Whatever exactly it is, it is quite needlessly obscure.

As William Strunk Jr. and E. B. White remark in their classic *The Elements of Style*, "[M]uddiness is not merely a disturber of prose, it is also a destroyer of life, of hope: death on the highway caused by a badly worded road sign, heartbreak among lovers caused by a misplaced phrase in a well-intentioned letter. . . ."[3] Only by paying careful attention to language can we avoid such needless miscommunications and disappointments.

> Confusion has its costs.
>
> —Crosby, Stills, and Nash

Critical thinkers not only strive for clarity of language but also seek maximum clarity of thought. As self-help books constantly remind us, to achieve our personal goals in life we need a clear conception of our goals and priorities, a realistic grasp of our abilities, and a clear understanding of the problems and opportunities we face. Such self-understanding can be achieved only if we value and pursue clarity of thought.

> Clarity is not a mere embellishment of the intellect; it is the very heart of intellectual virtue.
>
> —Charles Larmore

Precision

Detective stories contain some of the most interesting examples of critical thinking in fiction. The most famous fictional sleuth is, of course, Sherlock Holmes, the immortal creation of British writer Sir Arthur Conan Doyle. In Doyle's stories Holmes is often able to solve complex mysteries when the bungling detectives from Scotland Yard haven't so much as a clue. What is the secret of his success? An extraordinary commitment to *precision*. First, by careful and highly trained observation, Holmes is able to discover clues that others have overlooked. Then, by a process of precise logical inference, he is able to reason from those clues to discover the solution to the mystery.

> Really valuable ideas can only be had at the price of close attention.
>
> —Charles S. Peirce

Everyone recognizes the importance of precision in specialized fields such as medicine, mathematics, architecture, and engineering. Critical thinkers also understand the importance of precise thinking in daily life. They understand that to cut through the confusions and uncertainties that surround many everyday problems and issues, it is often necessary to insist on precise answers to precise questions: What exactly is the problem we're facing? What exactly are the alternatives? What exactly are the advantages and disadvantages of each alternative? Only when we habitually seek such precision are we truly critical thinkers.

Accuracy

There is a well-known saying about computers: "Garbage in, garbage out." Simply put, this means that if you put bad information into a computer, bad information is exactly what you will get out of it. Much the same is true of human thinking. No matter how brilliant you may be, you're almost guaranteed to make bad decisions if your decisions are based on false information.

A good example of this is provided by America's long and costly involvement in Vietnam. The policymakers who embroiled us in that conflict were not stupid. On the contrary, they were, in journalist David Halberstam's oft-quoted phrase, "the best and the brightest" of their generation. Of course, the reasons for their repeated failures of judgment are

> No one can navigate well through life without an accurate map by which to steer. Knowledge is the possession of such a map, and truth is what the map gives us, linking us to reality.
>
> —Tom Morris

complex and controversial; but much of the blame, historians agree, must be placed on false and inadequate information: ignorance of Vietnamese history and culture, an exaggerated estimate of the strategic importance of Vietnam and Southeast Asia, false assumptions about the degree of popular support in South Vietnam, unduly optimistic assessments of the "progress" of the war, and so on. Had American policymakers taken greater pains to learn the truth about such matters, it is likely they would not have made the poor decisions they did.

Critical thinkers don't merely value the truth; they have a *passion* for accurate, timely information. As consumers, citizens, workers, and parents, they strive to make decisions that are as informed as possible. In the spirit of Socrates' famous statement that the unexamined life is not worth living, they never stop learning, growing, and inquiring.

Relevance

Anyone who has ever sat through a boring school assembly or watched a mud-slinging political debate can appreciate the importance of staying focused on relevant ideas and information. A favorite debaters' trick is to try to distract an audience's attention by raising an irrelevant issue. Even Abraham Lincoln wasn't above such tricks, as the following story told by his law partner illustrates:

> *In a case where Judge [Stephen T.] Logan—always earnest and grave—opposed him, Lincoln created no little merriment by his reference to Logan's style of dress. He carried the surprise in store for the latter, till he reached his turn before the jury. Addressing them, he said: "Gentlemen, you must be careful and not permit yourselves to be overcome by the eloquence of counsel for the defense. Judge Logan, I know, is an effective lawyer. I have met him too often to doubt that; but shrewd and careful though he be, still he is sometimes wrong. Since this trial has begun I have discovered that, with all his caution and fastidiousness, he hasn't knowledge enough to put his shirt on right."*
>
> *Logan turned red as crimson, but sure enough, Lincoln was correct, for the former had donned a new shirt, and by mistake had drawn it over his head with the pleated bosom behind. The general laugh which followed destroyed the effect of Logans eloquence over the jury—the very point at which Lincoln aimed.*

> No tedious and irrelevant discussion can be allowed; what is said should be pertinent.
>
> —Plato

Lincoln's ploy was entertaining and succeeded in distracting the attention of the jury. Had the jurors been thinking critically, however, they would have realized that carelessness about one's attire has no logical relevance to the strength of one's arguments.

Consistency

It is easy to see why consistency is essential to critical thinking. Logic tells us that if a person holds inconsistent beliefs, at least one of those beliefs must be false. Critical thinkers prize truth and so are constantly on the lookout for inconsistencies, both in their oven thinking and in the arguments and assertions of others.

There are two kinds of inconsistency that we should avoid. One is *logical inconsistency*, which involves saying or believing inconsistent things (i.e., things that cannot both or all be true) about a particular matter. The other is *practical inconsistency*, which involves saying one thing and doing another.

Sometimes people are fully aware that their words conflict with their deeds. The politician who cynically breaks her campaign promises once she takes office, the TV evangelist caught in an extramarital affair, the drug counselor arrested for peddling drugs—such people are hypocrites pure and simple. From a critical thinking point of view, such examples are not especially interesting. As a rule, they involve failures of character to a greater degree than they do failures of critical reasoning.

> The guiding principle of rational behavior is consistency.
>
> —Deborah J. Bennett

More interesting from a critical thinking standpoint are cases in which people are not fully aware that their words conflict with their deeds. Such cases highlight an important lesson of critical thinking: that human beings often display a remarkable capacity for self-deception. Author Harold Kushner cites an all-too-typical example:

> Ask the average person which is more important to him, making money or being devoted to his family and virtually everyone will answer family without hesitation. But watch how the average person actually lives out his life. See where he really invests his time and energy, and he will give away the fact that he really does not live by what he says he believes. He has let himself be persuaded that if he leaves for work earlier in the morning and comes home more tired at night, he is proving how devoted he is to his family by expending himself to provide them with all the things they have seen advertised.

Speaking of Inconsistency . . .

Philosophy professor Kenneth R. Merrill offers the following tongue-in-cheek advice for writers. What kind of inconsistency does Merrill commit?

1. Watch your spelling. Writters who mispele a lott of words are propperly reguarded as iliterate.

2. Don't forget the apostrophe where its needed, but don't stick it in where theres no need for it. A writers reputation hangs on such trifle's.

3. Don't exaggerate. Overstatement always causes infinite harm.

4. Beware of the dangling participle. Forgetting this admonition, infelicitous phrases creep into our writing.

5. Cliches should be avoided like the plague. However, hackneyed language is not likely to be a problem for the writer who, since he was knee-high to a grasshopper, has built a better mousetrap and has kept his shoulder to the wheel.

6. Keep your language simple. Eschew sesquipedalian locutions and fustian rhetoric. Stay clear of the crepuscular—nay, tenebrific and fuliginous—regions of orotund sonorities.

7. Avoid vogue words. Hopefully, the writer will remember that her words basically impact the reader at the dynamic interface of creative thought and action. To be viable, the writer's parameters must enable her to engage the knowledgeable reader in a meaningful dialogue—especially at this point in time, when people tend to prioritize their priorities optimally.

8. Avoid profane or abusive language. It is a damned outrage how many knuckle-dragging slobs vilify people they disagree with.

Critical thinking helps us become aware of such unconscious practical inconsistencies, allowing us to deal with them on a conscious and rational basis.

It is also common, of course, for people to unknowingly hold inconsistent beliefs about a particular subject. In fact, as Socrates pointed out long ago, such unconscious logical inconsistency is far more common than most people suspect. As we shall see, for example, many today claim that "morality is relative," while holding a variety of views that imply that it is not relative. Critical thinking helps us recognize such logical inconsistencies or, still better, avoid them altogether.

Logical Correctness

To think logically is to reason correctly—that is, to draw well-founded conclusions from the beliefs we hold. To think critically we need accurate and well-supported beliefs. But, just as important, we need to be able to reason from those beliefs to conclusions that logically follow from them. Unfortunately, illogical thinking is all too common in human affairs. Bertrand Russell, in his classic essay "An Outline of Intellectual Rubbish," provides an amusing example:

I am sometimes shocked by the blasphemies of those who think themselves pious—for instance, the nuns who never take a bath without wearing a bathrobe all the time. When asked why, since no man can see them, they reply: "Oh, but you forget the good God." Apparently they conceive of the deity as a Peeping Tom, whose omnipotence enables Him to see through bathroom walls, but who is foiled by bathrobes. This view strikes me as curious.

As Russell observes, from the proposition

1. God sees everything.

the pious nuns correctly drew the conclusion

2. God sees through bathroom walls.

However, they failed to draw the equally obvious conclusion that

3. God sees through bathrobes.

Such illogic is, indeed, curious—but not, alas, uncommon.

> There is a difference between knowing the path and walking the path.
>
> —Morpheus, in The Matrix

> Intelligence means a person who can see implications and arrive at conclusions.
>
> —Talmud

> Man is the Reasoning Animal. Such is the claim. I think it is open to dispute. Indeed, my experiments have proven to me that he is the Unreasoning Animal. Note his history. . . . His record is the fantastic record of a maniac.
>
> —Mark Twain

Completeness

In most contexts, we rightly prefer deep and complete thinking to shallow and superficial thinking. Thus, we justly condemn slipshod criminal investigations, hasty jury deliberations, superficial news stories, sketchy driving directions, and snap medical diagnoses. Of course, there are times when it is impossible or inappropriate to discuss an issue in depth; no one would expect, for example, a thorough and wide-ranging discussion of the ethics of human genetic research in a short newspaper editorial. Generally speaking, however, thinking is better when it is deep rather than shallow, thorough rather than superficial.

Critical Thinking Lapse

The human race are masters of the ridiculous. There was actually a story in our newspaper of a man who was bitten on the tongue while kissing a rattlesnake. He decided to try a nonscientific remedy he heard about to counteract a snakebite. So he wired his mouth to a pickup truck battery and tried to jump-start his tongue. It knocked him out and he ended up in the hospital, where he lost part of his tongue and one lip.

Fairness

Finally, critical thinking demands that our thinking be fair—that is, open-minded, impartial, and free of distorting biases and pre-conceptions. That can be very difficult to achieve. Even the most superficial acquaintance with history and the social sciences tells us that people are often strongly disposed to resist unfamiliar ideas, to prejudge issues, to stereotype outsiders, and to identify truth with their own self-interest or the interests of their nation or group. It is probably unrealistic to suppose that our thinking could ever be completely free of biases and preconceptions; to some extent we all perceive reality in ways that are powerfully shaped by our individual life experiences and cultural backgrounds. But as difficult as it may be to achieve, basic fair-mindedness is clearly an essential attribute of a critical thinker.

> It is only when there is completeness and exhaustiveness that there is scholarship.
>
> —Hsün Tzu

> It is not much good thinking of a thing unless you think it out.
>
> —H. G. Wells

EXERCISE 1.1

I. Break into groups of four or five. Choose one member of your group to take notes and be the group reporter. Discuss your education up to this point. To what extent has your education prepared you to think clearly, precisely, accurately, logically, and so forth? Have you ever known a person (e.g., a teacher or a parent) who strongly modeled the critical thinking standards discussed in this section? If so, how did he or she do that?

II. Have you ever been guilty of either practical inconsistency (saying one thing and doing another) or logical inconsistency (believing inconsistent things about a particular topic or issue)? In small groups think of examples either from your own experience or from that of someone you know. Be prepared to share your examples with the class as a whole.

> Closed-mindedness means premature intellectual old age.
>
> —John Dewey

The Benefits of Critical Thinking

Having looked at some of the key intellectual standards governing critical reasoning (clarity, precision, and so forth), let's now consider more specifically what you can expect to gain from a course in critical thinking.

Critical Thinking in the Classroom

When they first enter college, students are sometimes surprised to discover that their professors seem less interested in how they got their beliefs than they are in whether those beliefs can withstand critical scrutiny. In college the focus is on higher-order thinking: the active, intelligent evaluation of ideas and information. For this reason critical thinking plays a vital role throughout the college curriculum.

> The main aim of education is practical and reflective judgment, a mind trained to be critical everywhere in the use of evidence.
>
> —Brand Blanchard

In a critical thinking course, students learn a variety of skills that can greatly improve their classroom performance. These skills include

- understanding the arguments and beliefs of others
- critically evaluating those arguments and beliefs
- developing and defending one's own well-supported arguments and beliefs

Let's look briefly at each of these three skills.

To succeed in college, you must, of course, be able to *understand* the material you are studying. A course in critical thinking cannot make inherently difficult material easy to grasp, but critical thinking does teach a variety of skills that, with practice, can significantly improve your ability to understand the arguments and issues discussed in your college textbooks and classes.

> We don't want you to axiomatically accept the conventional wisdom on a particular subject. Indeed, your first instinct should be to question it.
>
> —John J. Mearsheimer

In addition, critical thinking can help you *critically evaluate* what you are learning in class. During your college career, your instructors will often ask you to discuss "critically" some argument or idea introduced in class. Critical thinking teaches a wide range of strategies and skills that can greatly improve your ability to engage in such critical evaluations.

You will also be asked to *develop your own arguments* on particular topics or issues. In an American Government class, for example, you might be asked to write a paper addressing the issue of whether Congress has gone too far in restricting presidential war powers. To write such a paper successfully, you must do more than simply find and assess relevant arguments and information. You must also be able to marshal arguments and evidence in a way that convincingly supports your view. The systematic training provided in a course in critical thinking can greatly improve that skill as well.

Critical Thinking in the Workplace

Surveys indicate that fewer than half of today's college graduates can expect to be working in their major field of study within five years of graduation. This statistic speaks volumes about changing workplace realities. Increasingly, employers are looking not for employees with highly specialized career skills, since such skills can usually best be learned on the job, but for employees with good thinking and communication skills—quick learners who can solve problems, think creatively, gather and analyze information, draw appropriate conclusions from data, and communicate their ideas clearly and effectively. These are exactly the kinds of generalized thinking and problem-solving skills that a course in critical thinking can improve.

Critical Thinking in Life

Critical thinking is valuable in many contexts outside the classroom and the workplace. Let's look briefly at three ways in which this is the case.

First, critical thinking can help us avoid making foolish personal decisions. All of us have at one time or another made decisions about consumer purchases, relationships, personal behavior, and the like that we later realized were seriously misguided or irrational. Critical thinking can help us avoid such mistakes by teaching us to think about important life decisions more carefully, clearly, and logically.

Second, critical thinking plays a vital role in promoting democratic processes. Despite what cynics might say, in a democracy it really is "we the people" who have the ultimate say over who governs and for what purposes. It is vital, therefore, that citizens' decisions be as informed and as deliberate as possible. Many of today's most serious societal problems—environmental destruction, nuclear proliferation, religious and ethnic intolerance, decaying inner cities, failing schools, spiraling health-care costs, to mention just a few— have largely been caused by poor critical thinking. And as Albert Einstein once remarked, "The significant problems we face cannot be solved at the level of thinking we were at when we created them."

Third, critical thinking is worth studying for its own sake, simply for the personal enrichment it can bring to our lives. One of the most basic truths of the human condition is that most people, most of the time, believe what they are told. Throughout most of recorded history, people accepted without question that the earth was the center of the universe, that demons cause disease, that slavery was just, and that women are inferior to men. Critical thinking, honestly and coura-geously pursued, can help free us from the unexamined assumptions and biases of our upbringing and our society. It lets us step back from the prevailing customs and ideologies of our culture and ask, "This is what I've been taught, but is it *true*? In short, critical thinking allows us to lead self-directed, "examined" lives. Such personal liberation is, as the word itself implies, the ultimate goal of a *liberal* arts educa-tion. Whatever other benefits it brings, a liberal education can have no greater reward.

> Communication skills, critical thinking skills, and writing skills are . . . the crucial attributes most employers value while hiring a potential employee.
>
> —The *Economic Times*

> Citizens who think for themselves, rather than uncritically ingesting what their leaders tell them, are the absolutely necessary ingredient of a society that is to remain truly free.
>
> —Howard Kahane

Barriers to Critical Thinking

The preceding section raises an obvious question: If critical thinking is so important, why is it that *uncritical* thinking is so common? Why is it that so many people—including many highly educated and intelligent people—find critical thinking so difficult?

The reasons, as you might expect, are quite complex. Here is a list of some of the most common barriers to critical thinking:

- lack of relevant background information
- poor reading skills
- bias
- prejudice
- superstition
- egocentrism (self-centered thinking)
- sociocentrism (group-centered thinking)
- peer pressure
- conformism
- provincialism (narrow, unsophisticated thinking)
- narrow-mindedness
- closed-mindedness
- distrust in reason
- relativistic thinking
- stereotyping
- unwarranted assumptions
- scapegoating (blaming the innocent)
- rationalization (inventing excuses to avoid facing our real motives)
- denial
- wishful thinking
- short-term thinking
- selective perception
- selective memory
- overpowering emotions
- self-deception
- face-saving (maintaining a good self-image)
- fear of change

Let's examine in detail five of these impediments—egocentrism, sociocentrism, unwarranted assumptions, relativistic thinking, and wishful thinking—that play an especially powerful role in hindering critical thinking.

Egocentrism

Egocentrism is the tendency to see reality as centered on oneself. Egocentrics are selfish, self-absorbed people who view their interests, ideas, and values as superior to everyone else's. All of us are affected to some degree by egocentric biases.

Egocentrism can manifest itself in a variety of ways. Two common forms are self-interested thinking and the superiority bias.

Self-interested thinking is the tendency to accept and defend beliefs that harmonize with one's self-interest. Almost no one is immune to self-interested thinking. Most doctors support legislation making it more difficult for them to be sued for malpractice; most lawyers do not. Most state university professors strongly support tenure, paid sabbaticals, low teaching loads, and a strong faculty voice in university governance; many state taxpayers and university administrators do not. Most factory workers support laws requiring advance notice of plant closings; most factory owners do not. Most American voters favor campaign finance reform; most elected politicians do not. Of course, some of these beliefs may be supported by good reasons. From a psychological standpoint, however, it is likely that self-interest plays at least some role in shaping the respective attitudes and beliefs.

> How quick come the reasons for approving what we like!
>
> —Jane Austen

Self-interested thinking, however understandable it may seem, is a major obstacle to critical thinking. Everyone finds it tempting at times to reason that "this benefits me, therefore it must be good"; but from a critical thinking standpoint, such "reasoning" is a sham. Implicit in such thinking is the assumption that "What is most important is what *I* want and need." But why should I, or anyone else, accept such an arbitrary and obviously self-serving assumption? What makes *your* wants and needs more important than everyone else's? Critical thinking condemns such special pleading. It demands that we weigh evidence and arguments objectively and impartially. Ultimately, it demands that we revere truth—even when it hurts.

> Admit your faults. I would if I had any.
>
> —Milton Berle

Superiority bias (also known as illusory superiority or the better-than-average effect) is the tendency to overrate oneself-—to see oneself as better in some respect than one actually is. We have all known braggarts or know-it-alls who claim to be more talented or knowledgeable than they really are. If you are like most people, you probably think of yourself as being an unusually self-aware person who is largely immune from any such self-deception. If so, then you too are probably suffering from superiority bias.

> The one thing that unites all human beings, regardless of age, gender, religion, economic status, or ethnic background, is that, deep down inside, we all believe that we are above-average drivers.
>
> —Dave Barry

Studies show that superiority bias is an extremely common trait. In one survey one million high school seniors were asked to rate themselves on their "ability to get along with others." Only 15 percent put themselves below the median. Other surveys have shown that 90 percent of business managers and more than 90 percent of college professors rate their performance as better than average. It is easy, of course, to understand why people tend to overrate themselves. We all like to feel good about ourselves. Nobody likes to think of himself or herself as being "below average" in some important respect. At the same time, however, it is important to be able to look honestly at our personal strengths and weaknesses. We want to set high personal goals, but not goals that are wildly unrealistic. Self-confidence grounded in genuine accomplishment is an important element of success. Overconfidence is an obstacle to genuine personal and intellectual growth.

Are you overconfident in your beliefs? Here's a simple test to determine if you are. For each of the following ten items, provide a low and a high guess such that you are 90 percent sure the correct answer falls between the two. Your challenge is to be neither too narrow (i.e., overconfident) nor too wide (i.e., underconfident). If you successfully meet the challenge, you should have 10 percent misses—that is, exactly one miss.

	90% Confidence Range	
	LOW	HIGH
1. Martin Luther King's age at death	————	————
2. Length of Nile River (in miles)	————	————
3. Percentage of African Americans in the United States	————	————
4. Number of books in the Old Testament	————	————
5. Diameter of the moon (in miles)	————	————
6. Weight of an empty Boeing 747 (in pounds)	————	————
7. Current population of California	————	————
8. Year in which Wolfgang Amadeus Mozart was born	————	————
9. Air distance from London to Tokyo (in miles)	————	————
10. Deepest known point in the ocean (in feet)	————	————

Sociocentrism

Sociocentrism is group-centered thinking. Just as egocentrism can hinder rational thinking by focusing excessively on the self, so sociocentrism can hinder rational thinking by focusing excessively on the group.

> He who knows most, knows best how little he knows.
>
> —Thomas Jefferson

Sociocentrism can distort critical thinking in many ways. Two of the most important are group bias and conformism.

Group bias is the tendency to see one's own group (nation, tribe, sect, peer group, and the like) as being inherently better than others. Social scientists tell us that such thinking is extremely common throughout human history and across cultures. Just as we seem naturally inclined to hold inflated views of ourselves, so we find it easy to hold inflated views of our family, our community, or our nation. Conversely, we find it easy to look with suspicion or disfavor on those we regard as "outsiders."

Most people absorb group bias unconsciously, usually from early childhood. It is common, for example, for people to grow up thinking that their society's beliefs, institutions, and values are better than those of other societies. Consider this exchange between eight-year-old Maurice D. and the well-known Swiss scientist and philosopher Jean Piaget:

Maurice D. (8 years, 3 months old): If you didn't have any nationality and you were given a free choice of nationality, which would you choose? Swiss nationality. *Why?* Because I was born in Switzerland. *Now look, do you think the French and the Swiss are equally nice, or the one nicer or less nice than the other?* The Swiss are nicer. *Why?* The French are always nasty. *Who is more intelligent, the Swiss or the French, or do you think they're just the same?* The Swiss are more intelligent. *Why?* Because they learn French quickly. *If I asked a French boy to choose any nationality he liked, what country do you think he'd choose?* He'd choose France. *Why?* Because he was born in France. *And what would he say about who's nicer? Would he think the Swiss and the French equally nice or one better than the other?* He'd say the French are nicer. *Why?* Because he was born in France. *And who would he think more intelligent?* The French. *Why?* He'd say that the French want to learn quicker than the Swiss. *Now you and the French boy don't really give the same answer. Who do you think answered best?* I did. *Why?* Because Switzerland is always better.

> Custom and example have a much more persuasive power than any certitude obtained by way of inquiry.
>
> —Rene Descartes

Pop Culture Connection

Poker and Critical Thinking

Poker players fall victim to critical thinking barriers like wishful thinking and self-serving bias just like anybody else. One barrier that can be particularly costly to poker players is overconfidence. Overconfident players think that they're better, or luckier, than they actually are. This often leads them to play with far superior opponents, to stay in too many hands, and to bet recklessly. The result: Players who overrate their abilities quickly become ATMs for their tablemates.

Poker legend Doyle Brunson tells a cautionary tale about the dangers of overconfidence. A cocky New Yorker calling himself "Rochester Ricky" and flashing a big bankroll walked into a Fort Worth poker parlor. Around the table sat Amarillo Slim, Puggy Pearson, Johnny Moss, Sailor Roberts, Brunson himself, and a couple of Texas businessmen. Two things quickly became apparent. Though he knew his game, Rochester hadn't played much no-limit poker, and he hadn't a clue he was playing against some of the best no-limit Hold'em poker talent in the world.

Rochester didn't realize that strategies that work well in limit games (for example, calling frequently and bluffing cautiously) often backfire in no-limit games. His parting words as he gathered up the paltry remnants of his $10,000 bankroll were "If you guys are ever in Rochester, don't bother to look me up. You won't see me playing Hold'em against Texans as long as I live."

As the great American philosopher Clint Eastwood said, "A man's got to know his limitations."

Although most people outgrow such childish nationalistic biases to some extent, few of us manage to outgrow them completely. Clearly, this kind of "mine-is-better" thinking lies at the root of a great deal of human conflict, intolerance, and oppression.

Conformism refers to our tendency to follow the crowd—that is, to conform (often unthinkingly) to authority or to group standards of conduct and belief. The desire to

> To those who would investigate the cause of existing opinions, the study of predispositions is much more important than the study of argument.
>
> —W. E. H. Lecky

belong, to be part of the in-group, can be among the most powerful of human motivations. As two classic experiments demonstrate, this desire to conform can seriously cripple our powers of critical reasoning and decision making.

In the first experiment, conducted in the 1950s by Solomon Asch, groups of eight college students were asked to match a standard line like the following ————————

with three comparison lines such as these:

A ——————

B ————————

C ——————

In each group, only one of the eight participants was unaware of the true nature of the experiment; the other seven were confederates working in league with the experimenter. In each case the single true subject was seated at the end of the table and asked to answer last. In some trials the seven confederates unanimously gave the correct answer (B); in others they unanimously gave an incorrect answer. The results: When no pressure to conform was present, subjects gave the correct answer more than 99 percent of the time. When faced with the united opposition of their peers, however, almost one-third (32 percent) of the subjects refused to believe their own eyes and gave answers that were obviously incorrect!

> When fifty million people say a foolish thing it is still a foolish thing.
> —Anatole France

Another famous experiment was conducted by Stanley Milgram in the 1960s. In Milgram's experiment, subjects were asked to administer a series of increasingly severe electrical shocks to people whom the subjects could hear but couldn't see. (In fact, no actual shocks were given; the shock "victims" were actually confederates who merely pretended to be in pain.) Subjects were told that they were participating in a study of the effects of punishment on learning. Their task was to act as "teachers" who inflicted progressively more painful shocks on "learners" whenever the latter failed to answer a question correctly. The severity of the shocks was controlled by a series of thirty switches, which ranged in 15-volt intervals from 15 volts ("Slight Shock") to 450 volts ("XX Danger: Severe Shock"). The purpose of the study was to determine how far ordinary people would go in inflicting pain on total strangers, simply because they were asked to do so by someone perceived to be "an authority."

> When all think alike, then no one is thinking.
> —Walter Lippmann

The results were, well, shocking. More than 85 percent of the subjects continued to administer shocks beyond the 300-volt mark, long after the point at which they could hear the victims crying out or pounding on the walls in pain. After the 330-volt mark, the screaming stopped, and for all the subjects knew, the victims were either unconscious or dead. Despite that, nearly two-thirds (65 percent) of the subjects continued to administer shocks, as they were instructed, until they had administered the maximum 450 volts.

> Man is born to think for himself.
> —Denis Diderot

The lesson of these studies is clear: "Authority moves us. We are impressed, influenced, and intimidated by authority, so much so that, under the right conditions, we abandon our own values, beliefs, and judgments, even doubt our own immediate sensory experience." As critical thinkers, we need to be aware of the seductive power of peer pressure and reliance on authority and develop habits of independent thinking to combat them.

Unwarranted Assumptions and Stereotypes

An **assumption** is something we take for granted, something we believe to be true without any proof or conclusive evidence. Almost everything we think and do is based on assumptions. If the weather report calls for rain, we take an umbrella because we assume that the meteorologist is not lying, that the report is based on a scientific analysis of weather patterns, that the instruments are accurate, and so forth. There may be no proof that any of this is true, but we realize that it is wiser to take the umbrella than to insist that the weather bureau provide exhaustive evidence to justify its prediction.

Although we often hear the injunction "Don't assume," it would be impossible to get through a day without making assumptions; in fact, many of our daily actions are based on assumptions we have drawn from the patterns in our experience. You go to class at the scheduled time because you assume that class is being held at its normal hour and in its same place. You don't call the professor each day to ask if class is being held; you just assume that it is. Such assumptions are *warranted*, which means that we have good reason to hold them. When you see a driver coming toward you with the turn signal on, you have good reason to believe that the driver intends to turn. You may be incorrect, and it might be safer to withhold action until you are certain, but your assumption is not unreasonable.

Unwarranted assumptions, however, are unreasonable. An *unwarranted* assumption is something taken for granted without good reason. Such assumptions often prevent our seeing things clearly. For example, our attraction for someone might cause us to assume that he or she feels the same way and thus to interpret that person's actions incorrectly.

One of the most common types of unwarranted assumptions is a **stereotype**. The word *stereotype* comes from the printing press era, when plates, or stereotypes, were used to produce identical copies of one page. Similarly, when we stereotype, as the word is now used, we assume that individual people have all been stamped from one plate, so all politicians are alike, or Muslims, or African Americans, professors, women, and so forth. When we form an opinion of someone that is based not on his or her individual qualities but, rather, on his or her membership in a particular group, we are assuming that all or virtually all members of that group are alike. Because people are not identical, no matter what race or other similarities they share, stereotypical conceptions will often be false or misleading.

Typically, stereotypes are arrived at through a process known as *hasty generalization*, in which one draws a conclusion about a large class of things (in this case, people) from a small sample. If we meet one South Bergian who is rude, we might jump to the conclusion that all South Bergians are rude. Or we might generalize from what we have heard from a few friends or read in a single news story. Often the media—advertisements, the news, movies, and so forth—encourage stereotyping by the way they portray groups of people.

> General notions are generally wrong.
>
> —Mary Worthley Montague

The assumptions we need to become most conscious of are not the ones that lead to our routine behaviors, such as carrying an umbrella or going to class, but the ones on which we base our more important attitudes, actions, and decisions. If we are conscious of our tendency to stereotype, we can take measures to end it.

I. Read this story and answer the questions that follow.

When it happened, a disturbing mix of feelings bubbled inside you. It sickened you to watch the boat slip beneath the waves and disappear forever; so much work had gone into maintaining it and keeping it afloat, but at least everyone was safe in the tiny lifeboat you'd had just enough time to launch. You secretly congratulated yourself for having had the foresight to stock the lifeboat with a few emergency items, such as a small amount of food and water, but you knew that a boat built to hold three, maybe four people wasn't going to survive too long with such an overload of passengers.

You looked around at your companions: the brilliant Dr. Brown, whose cleverness and quick wit had impressed you on many occasions; Marie Brown, pregnant and clearly exhausted from the climb into the lifeboat; Lieutenant Ashley Morganstern, a twenty-year veteran who'd seen the most brutal sorts of combat; the lieutenant's secretary and traveling companion, whose shirt you noticed for the first time bore the monogram LB, but whom everyone called, simply, "Letty"; and Eagle-Eye Sam, the trusted friend who'd been at your side for many years as you sailed the oceans in your precious, now-vanished boat and whose nickname came from his ability to spot the smallest objects seemingly miles away at sea.

Seeing the fear on your passengers' faces, you tried to comfort them: "Don't worry; we'll be fine. They'll be looking for us right away. I'm sure of it." But you weren't so sure. In fact, you knew it wasn't true. It might be days before you were found, since you'd had no time to radio for help. Rescuers probably wouldn't be dispatched until Friday, five days from now, when your failure to show up in port would finally arouse concern.

On the third day, your passengers showed increasing signs of frustration, anger, and fear. "Where are they?" Marie cried. "We can't go on like this!"

You knew she was right. *We can't*, you thought, *not all of us anyway.*

On the fourth day, the food was completely gone, and just enough water remained to keep per-haps three people alive for another day, maybe two. Suddenly, things got worse. "Is that water?!" Marie screamed, pointing a shaking finger at the bottom of the lifeboat. Horrified, you looked down to see a slight trickle of water seeping in at the very center of the boat. Dr. Brown grabbed a T-shirt that was lying in the bottom of the boat and used it like a sponge to absorb the water, wringing it out over the side and plunging it into the invading water again and again. But it was no use; the water began to seep in faster than Brown could work.

"We're too heavy," the lieutenant insisted without emotion. "We've got to lighten the load. Some-one has to get out and swim."

"Swim?!" Marie gasped in disbelief. "Are you insane?! There are sharks in these waters!"

"Who's it going to be, Captain?" the lieutenant asked almost coldly, staring you square in the eye. "Which one of us swims?"

"Me. I'll go," you say, swinging your leg out over the side of the boat.

"No," Letty insisted. "You're the only one who knows how to navigate. If you go, we'll all die. You must choose one of us to sacrifice."

And so you did.

A. Answer the following questions individually.

1. Which one did you choose? Why? Why didn't you choose the others?

2. As you read, you probably imagined what the characters looked like. From the image you had of them, describe the following characters in a few sentences:

The Captain

Dr. Brown

Marie Brown

Lieutenant Ashley Morganstern

Letty

Eagle-Eye Sam

3. Do you think Dr. Brown is related to Marie Brown? If so, how?

B. Now form groups of three and complete the following tasks:

1. Compare your responses to question 1 in part A. Discuss the reasons for your decisions. Is there any consensus in the group?

2. Do you all agree on the relationship between Dr. Brown and Marie Brown?

3. What evidence is there in the story to support your answer for question 3 in part A? Is it possible that they are related in another way or not at all?

4. Look at your portraits of Dr. Brown. How many assumptions did you and your group members make about the doctor's gender, age, appearance, and profession? What evidence in the story supports your image of the doctor? If your images are similar, what do you think accounts for that similarity? Are your mental images similar to ones we normally see in the media, for example?

5. Look at your portraits of the other characters. First, what similarities do you find among your group's members? Second, what evidence is there in the story to support your assumptions? Are other assumptions possible? Finally, where do you think your mental images came from?

II. In groups of three or four, name and explain a stereotypical conception people may have had about you over the years. Note how that stereotypical conception keeps others from coming to know you more accurately. Turn your page over and exchange papers with other members of your group. See if the other members can determine which stereotype description goes with what member of your group.

Relativistic Thinking

Virtually every college professor has had at least one conversation like the following:

Janie: Professor X, I don't understand why you gave me a D on this paper.

Prof. X: Well, as I noted in my written comments, you state your opinions, but you don't offer any reasons to back them up.

Janie: Do you mean you gave me a low grade because you disagree with my opinions?

Prof. X: No, not at all, Janie. You received a low grade because you didn't give any reasons to support your opinions.

Janie: But isn't everyone entitled to his or her own opinion? And can anyone ever really prove that his or her opinion is right and everyone else's is wrong? Why, then, do I have to give reasons for my opinions when I'm entitled to hold them and no one can prove that they're wrong?

Janie, here, has fallen into the trap of *relativistic thinking*. It is crucial to understand -why this is a trap, because once one has fallen into it, it is very difficult to see any point in studying critical thinking at all.

Relativism is the view that truth is a matter of opinion. There are two popular forms of relativism: subjectivism and cultural relativism. **Subjectivism** is the view that truth is a matter of individual opinion. This is the view Janie apparently holds. According to subjectivism, whatever an individual believes is true, *is* true for that person, and there is no such thing as "objective" or "absolute" truth, i.e., truth that exists independent of what anyone believes. For example, suppose Bobby believes that abortion is wrong and Alice believes that abortion is not always -wrong. According to subjectivism, abortion is always wrong for Bobby and not always wrong for Alice. Both beliefs are true—*for them*. And truth *for* one individual or another is the only kind of truth there is.

The other common form of relativism is **cultural relativism**. This is the view that truth is a matter of social or cultural opinion. In other words, cultural relativism is the view that what is true for person A is what person A's culture or society believes is true. Drinking wine, for example, is widely considered to be wrong in Iran but is not generally considered to be wrong in France. According to cultural relativism, therefore, drinking wine is immoral in Iran but is morally permissible in France. Thus, for the cultural relativist, just as for the subjectivist, there is no objective or absolute standard of truth. What is true is whatever most people in a society or culture believe to be true.

Relatively few people endorse subjectivism or cultural relativism in the pure, unqualified forms in which we have stated them. Almost everybody would admit, for example, that 1 + 1 = 2 is true, no matter who might be ignorant or deluded enough to deny it. What relativists usually claim, therefore, is not that all truth is relative, but that truth is relative in some important domain(s). By far the most common form of relativism is *moral relativism*. Like relativism generally, moral relativism comes in two major forms: moral subjectivism and cultural moral relativism. **Moral subjectivism** is the view that what is morally right and good for an individual, A, is whatever A believes is morally right and good. Thus, if Andy believes that premarital sex is always wrong, and Jennifer believes that it is not always wrong, according to moral subjectivism premarital sex is always wrong for Andy and is not always wrong for Jennifer.

The other major form of moral relativism is **cultural moral relativism**, the view that what is morally right and good for an individual, A, is whatever A's society or culture believes is morally right and good. Thus, according to cultural moral relativism, if culture A believes that polygamy is wrong, and culture B believes that polygamy is right, then polygamy is wrong for culture A and right for culture B.

Cultural moral relativism is a very popular view today, especially among the young. There are two major reasons people seem to find it so attractive. One has to do with the nature of moral disagreement, and the other concerns the value of tolerance.

Ethics, obviously, is very different from math or science. In math and science, there are arguments and disagreements, but not nearly to the extent there are in ethics. In ethics there is widespread disagreement, the disagreements often go very deep, and there seems to be no rational way to resolve many of them. What this shows, some people conclude, is that there is no objective truth in ethics; morality is just a matter of individual or societal opinion.

Another reason people find cultural moral relativism attractive is that it seems to support the value of tolerance. Throughout history, terrible wars, persecutions, and acts of religious and cultural imperialism have been perpetrated by people who firmly believed in the absolute righteousness of their moral beliefs and practices. Cultural moral relativism seems to imply that we must be tolerant of other cultures' moral beliefs and values. If culture A believes that polygamy is wrong, and culture B believes that it is right, then culture A must agree that polygamy is right for culture B, no matter how offensive the practice may be to culture A.

Despite these apparent attractions, however, there are deep problems with cultural moral relativism, as the following exercise (adapted from a set of role-playing scenarios developed by Professor Grant H. Cornwell) will illustrate.

EXERCISE 1.4

In groups of four or five, choose a group reporter to take notes and be the group spokesperson. Read and discuss one of the following case studies as assigned by your instructor.

Case 1

Definition: A cultural moral relativist is one who maintains the following thesis: *Whatever members of a culture believe is morally right and good is morally right and good for them.*

You are a member of culture C studying cultures A and B. You are a committed cultural moral relativist, i.e., you maintain wholeheartedly the relativist thesis.

Culture A is a pacifist culture and believes that it is always morally wrong to commit a violent act against another human being for any reason. Culture B is a militaristic and slaveholding culture. Its members believe that it is morally good and right to invade, subjugate, and enslave other cultures. While you are observing them, culture B invades culture A.

DISCUSSION QUESTIONS

1. What can you consistently believe with regard to the morality of culture A? The morality of culture B? Specifically, as a consistent moral relativist, can you criticize or condemn the morality of culture A? Of culture B?

2. What can you consistently do with regard to culture B's invasion and attempted subjugation of culture A?

Case 2

Definition: A cultural moral relativist is one who maintains the following thesis: *Whatever members of a culture believe is morally right and good is morally right and good for them.*

You are a member of culture B and a committed cultural moral relativist, i.e., you maintain wholeheartedly the relativist thesis.

Culture B is a militaristic and slaveholding culture. A majority of its members believe that it is morally right and good to invade, subjugate, and enslave other cultures.

Culture A is a pacifist culture. A majority of its members believe that it is always wrong to commit any act of violence against another human being for any reason.

Culture B believes that it is morally wrong for culture A to practice pacifism. Culture B invades culture A. Its aim is to subjugate and enslave members of culture A and force some of them to participate in gladiatorial bouts for the amusement of members of culture B.

DISCUSSION QUESTIONS

1. Is there any logical inconsistency in being a cultural moral relativist and also belonging to culture B? (*Hint*: Consider not only what culture B believes is right and good for its own members to do but also what it believes is right and good for other cultures to do.) If so, which beliefs, precisely, are inconsistent?

2. What can you consistently believe with regard to the morality of culture A? The morality of culture B? Specifically, as a consistent moral relativist, can you criticize or condemn the morality of culture A? Of culture B?

3. What can you consistently do with regard to culture B's invasion and attempted conquest of culture A?

Case 3

Definition: A cultural moral relativist is one who maintains the following thesis: *Whatever members of a culture believe is morally right and good is morally right and good for them.*

Culture B consists of two subcultures: the Alphas and the Betas. The Alphas are a ruling majority group. They believe that it is morally right to randomly select a young child for sacrifice at the beginning of each year. The Betas are an oppressed minority group with its own distinctive cultural, moral, and religious practices. Betas believe strongly that child sacrifice is morally wrong.

You are a member of culture B and a Beta. You are also a committed cultural moral relativist, i.e., you maintain wholeheartedly the relativist thesis. Culture A is a pacifist culture. Members of this culture believe that it is always wrong to commit any act of violence against another human being for any reason.

The Alphas believe that it is morally right to impose their beliefs and values on culture A. They believe that it is a moral atrocity that culture A does not sacrifice children, and they believe that they have a moral duty to use whatever means are necessary to change the beliefs of culture A and have its members comply with this practice.

Culture B invades culture A and begins its program of subjugation and indoctrination.

DISCUSSION QUESTIONS

1. Is it possible for an individual to belong to more than one culture at the same time? If so, does this pose any logical difficulty for the cultural moral relativist?

2. Is there any logical difficulty in being a moral relativist and belonging to culture B? (*Hint:* Consider not only what culture B believes is right and good for its own members to do but also what it believes is right and good for other cultures to do.)

3. What can you consistently believe with regard to the morality of culture A? The morality of culture B? Specifically, as a consistent moral relativist, can you criticize or condemn the morality of culture A? Of culture B?

4. What can you consistently do with regard to culture B's invasion and attempted subjugation of culture A?

5. Suppose that sometime in the future the Betas become the majority subculture in culture B, and a majority of culture B comes to believe that child sacrifice is wrong. Can this be described as "moral progress" from the standpoint of cultural moral relativism? Why or why not?

These cases highlight several serious problems with cultural moral relativism.

1. *Relativism makes it impossible for us to criticize other cultures' customs and values, even those that intuitively seem to us to be terribly wrong.* We can no longer say, for example, that a particular culture is wrong to practice slavery or child sacrifice, as long as that culture believes that those practices are morally right.

2. *Relativism makes it impossible for us to criticize our own societies' customs and values.* Suppose you personally oppose racial segregation, but a majority of your society supports it. According to relativism, you must change your mind and agree that racial segregation is right in your society. In fact, if relativism is true, anyone who criticizes majority values is always wrong. Total conformity to majority opinion is required.

3. *Relativism rules out the idea of moral progress.* Moral values can change, but if relativism is true, they can never become better or worse, for relativism implies that what is right

for a society is what that culture believes is right at that time. Thus, a relativist cannot say, for example, that the abolition of slavery or laws outlawing gender discrimination represented moral progress in the United States.

4. *Relativism can lead to conflicting moral duties.* There are several ways in which a relativist might find himself stuck with conflicting moral beliefs and duties. Cases 2 and 3 highlight two ways in which this can occur:

   a. *When a relativist is a member of a society that holds beliefs that conflict with moral relativism* (cases 2 and 3). If your society believes, for example, that child sacrifice is absolutely and objectively right, then you too, as a moral relativist, must believe that child sacrifice is absolutely and objectively right, for whatever moral beliefs your society holds, you must hold as well.

   b. *When a relativist belongs to two or more cultures and those cultures hold mutually inconsistent moral beliefs* (case 3). Can a person belong to two different cultures at the same time? It is hard to see why not. An Amish farmer living in Ohio, for instance, would seem to be a member of both an Amish culture and a larger American one. If such dual membership is possible, however, conflicts can clearly occur between the two cultures' moral codes. And given relativism's claim that what is right for a person is whatever his or her culture believes is right, this could lead to conflicting moral duties.

Thus, cultural moral relativism has consequences that make it very difficult to accept. In addition, however, it can be shown that the two main reasons people are attracted to cultural moral relativism—ethical disagreement and the value of tolerance—are not good reasons at all.

First, does the fact that there is deep disagreement in ethics show that there is no objective moral truth—that ethics is just a matter of opinion? Hardly. Think about another area in which there is deep, pervasive, and seemingly irresolvable disagreement: religion. People disagree vehemently over whether God exists, whether there is an afterlife, and so forth; yet we don't conclude from this that there is no objective truth about these matters. It may be difficult to *know* whether God exists. But *whether* he exists is not simply a matter of opinion. Thus, deep disagreement about an issue does not show that there is no objective truth about that issue.

Second, as the cases in Exercise 1.4 make clear, cultural moral relativism does not necessarily support the value of tolerance. Relativism tells us that we should accept the customs and values of our society. Thus, if you live in an intolerant society, relativism implies that you too should be intolerant.

> We all need to be a little humble in our certainties.
> —Tom Morris

Does this mean that cultural moral relativism has nothing at all to teach us? No. The fact that people disagree so much about ethics does not show that moral truth is simply a matter of opinion, but it should make us cautious and open-minded regarding our own ethical beliefs. If millions of obviously decent, intelligent people disagree with you, how can you be sure that your values are the correct ones? In this way relativism can teach us an important lesson about the value of intellectual humility. But we don't need relativism—which is a false and confused theory—to teach us this lesson. We can learn it just by opening our hearts and minds and thinking critically about the challenges of living an ethical life.

Wishful Thinking

> The easiest thing of all is to deceive one's self; for what a man wishes, he generally believes to be true.
>
> —Demosthenes

> A man hears what he wants to hear and disregards the rest.
>
> —Paul Simon

> The universe is what it is, not what I choose that it should be.
>
> —Bertrand Russell

Once, as a Little Leaguer, one of the authors was thrown out at the plate in a foolish attempt to stretch a triple into a home run, possibly costing the team the game. Angry and disappointed, he refused to believe that he had really been thrown out. "I was safe by a mile," he said plaintively to his disbelieving coaches and teammates. It was only years later, when he was an adult, that he could admit to himself that he really had been out—out, in fact, by a mile.

Have you ever been guilty of wishful thinking—believing something not because you had good evidence for it but simply because you wished it were true? If so, you're not alone. Throughout human history, reason has done battle with wishful thinking and has usually come out the loser.

People fear the unknown and invent comforting myths to render the universe less hostile and more predictable. They fear death and listen credulously to stories of healing crystals, quack cures, and communication with the dead. They fantasize about possessing extraordinary personal powers and accept uncritically accounts of psychic prediction, levitation, and ESP. They delight in tales of the marvelous and the uncanny, and they buy mass-market tabloids that feature headlines such as "Spiritual Sex Channeler: Medium Helps Grieving Widows Make Love to their Dead Husbands." They kid themselves into thinking, "It can't happen to me," and then find themselves dealing with the consequences of unwanted pregnancies, drunk-driving convictions, drug addiction, or AIDS.

EXERCISE 1.5

I. Have you ever been guilty of self-interested thinking, self-serving bias, group bias, conformism, or wishful thinking? Without embarrassing yourself too much, discuss these critical thinking lapses in groups of three or four, then share with the class whatever examples you'd like to discuss.

II. This textbook gives a number of examples of self-interested thinking, self-serving bias, group bias, conformism, and wishful thinking. Jot down at least two additional examples of each of these five critical thinking hindrances. Divide into groups of three or four, discuss your examples with the group, and share what you think are the best examples with the class as a whole.

Characteristics of a Critical Thinker

So far in this chapter, we have discussed (1) the nature of critical thinking; (2) key critical thinking standards such as clarity, precision, accuracy, and fairness; (3) the benefits of critical thinking; and (4) some major impediments to critical thinking, including egocentrism, sociocentrism, relativistic thinking, unwarranted assumptions, and wishful thinking. With this as background, we are now in a position to offer a general profile of a critical thinker. The following list contrasts some of the key intellectual traits of critical thinkers with the relevant traits of uncritical thinkers.

Critical Thinkers . . .

Have a passionate drive for clarity precision, accuracy, and other critical thinking standards.

Are sensitive to ways in which critical thinking can be skewed by egocentrism, sociocentrism, wishful thinking, and other impediments.

Are skilled at understanding, analyzing, and evaluating arguments and viewpoints.

Reason logically and draw appropriate conclusions from evidence and data.

Are intellectually honest with themselves, acknowledging what they don't know and recognizing their limitations.

Listen open-mindedly to opposing points of view and welcome criticisms of beliefs and assumptions.

Base their beliefs on facts and evidence rather than on personal preference or self-interest.

Are aware of the biases and preconceptions that shape the way they perceive the world.

Think independently and are not afraid to disagree with group opinion.

Are able to get to the heart of an issue or a problem, without being distracted by details.

Have the intellectual courage to face and assess fairly ideas that challenge even their most basic beliefs.

Pursue truth and are curious about a wide range of issues.

Have the intellectual perseverance to pursue insights or truths despite obstacles or difficulties.

Uncritical Thinkers . . .

Often think in ways that are unclear, imprecise, and inaccurate.

Often fall prey to egocentrism, sociocentrism, relativistic thinking, unwarranted assumptions, and wishful thinking.

Often misunderstand or evaluate unfairly arguments and viewpoints.

Think illogically and draw unsupported conclusions from evidence and data.

Pretend they know more than they do and ignore their limitations.

Are closed-minded and resist criticisms of beliefs and assumptions.

Often base beliefs on mere personal preference or self-interest.

Lack awareness of their own biases and preconceptions.

Tend to engage in "groupthink," uncritically following the beliefs and values of the crowd.

> What is the hardest task in the world? To think.
>
> —Ralph Waldo Emerson

Are easily distracted and lack the ability to zero in on the essence of an issue or a problem.

Fear and resist ideas that challenge their basic beliefs.

Are often relatively indifferent to truth and lack curiosity.

Tend not to persevere when they encounter intellectual obstacles or difficulties.

> Character is destiny.
>
> —Heraclitus

A course in critical thinking is like most other things in life: You get out of it what you put into it. If you approach critical thinking as a chore—a pointless general education requirement you need to get out of the way before you can turn to more "relevant" courses in your major—a chore it will be. On the other hand, if you approach critical thinking as an

> To become a critical thinker is not, in the end, to be the same person you are now, only with better abilities; it is, in an important sense, to become a different person.
> —Gerald Nosich

opportunity to learn habits of disciplined thinking that are vital to success in school, in your career, and in your life as a liberally educated person, critical thinking can be a rewarding and even transformative experience.

Exercise 1.6

I. Review the list of critical thinking traits above, then write a 250-word essay in which you address the following questions: Which of the traits listed do you think is your strongest critical thinking trait? Why? Which is your weakest? Why? What could you do to improve in this latter regard? Be specific and realistic.

II. In groups of three or four, define the following critical thinking traits: intellectual honesty, open-mindedness, fair-mindedness, intellectual courage, and intellectual perseverance. (See the list of critical thinking traits above for some broad hints.) Give an example of each.

III. In groups of three or four, think of examples, either from your experience or from your knowledge of current events or history, of individuals who possess, or did possess, the quality of intellectual courage to an unusual degree. What about them leads you to think of them as being especially intellectually courageous? Do the same for the qualities of open-mindedness, intellectual honesty, and intellectual perseverance. Be prepared to share your group's best examples with the class.

Summary

1. *Critical thinking* is the general term given to a wide range of cognitive skills and intellectual dispositions needed to effectively identify, analyze, and evaluate arguments and truth claims; to discover and overcome personal preconceptions and biases; to formulate and present convincing reasons in support of conclusions; and to make reasonable, intelligent decisions about what to believe and what to do. It is disciplined thinking governed by clear intellectual standards that have proven their value over the course of human history. Among the most important of these intellectual standards are clarity, precision, accuracy, relevance, consistency, logical correctness, completeness, and fairness.

2. Critical thinking is beneficial for many reasons. It can help students do better in school by improving their ability to understand, construct, and criticize arguments. It can help people succeed in their careers by improving their ability to solve problems, think creatively, and communicate their ideas clearly and effectively. It can also reduce the likelihood of making serious mistakes in important personal decisions, promote democratic processes by improving the quality of public decision making, and liberate and empower individuals by freeing them from the unexamined assumptions, dogmas, and prejudices of their upbringing, their society, and their age.

3. Major barriers to critical thinking include egocentrism, sociocentrism, unwarranted assumptions, relativistic thinking, and wishful thinking.

   Egocentrism is the tendency to see reality as centered on oneself. Two common forms of egocentrism are self-interested thinking (the tendency to accept and defend beliefs that accord with one's own self-interest) and the superiority bias (the tendency to overrate oneself).

   Sociocentrism is group-centered thinking. Two common varieties of sociocentrism are group bias (the tendency to see one's culture or group as being better than others) and conformism (the tendency to conform, often unthinkingly, to authority or to group standards of conduct and belief).

Unwarranted assumptions are things we take for granted without good reason. Often, unwarranted assumptions take the form of stereotypes. Stereotypes are generalizations about a group of people in which identical characteristics are assigned to all or virtually all members of the group, often without regard to whether such attributions are accurate.

To learn is to face transformation . . .
—Parker J. Palmer

Relativistic thinking is thinking that is based on the idea that there is no "objective" or "absolute" truth because truth is simply a matter of opinion. The most popular form of relativism is *moral relativism*, which holds that what is morally right and good varies from individual to individual (*moral subjectivism*) or from culture to culture (*cultural moral relativism*).

Wishful thinking is believing something because it makes one feel good, not because there is good reason for thinking that it is true.

4. Critical thinkers exhibit a number of traits that distinguish them from uncritical thinkers. Among the most important of these traits are a passionate drive for clarity, precision, accuracy, and other intellectual standards that characterize careful, disciplined thinking; a sensitivity to the ways in which critical thinking can be skewed by egocentrism, wishful thinking, and other psychological obstacles to rational belief; honesty and intellectual humility; open-mindedness; intellectual courage; love of truth; and intellectual perseverance.

Chapter 2: Recognizing Arguments and Reasoning

Recognizing Arguments

Gregory Bassham et al

As we saw in the previous chapter, critical thinking is centrally concerned with reasons: identifying reasons, evaluating reasons, and giving reasons. In critical thinking, passages that present reasons for a claim are called *arguments*. In this chapter we explore the concept of an argument and explain how to distinguish arguments from nonarguments.

What Is an Argument?

When people hear the word *argument*, they usually think of some kind of quarrel or shouting match. In critical thinking, however, an argument is simply a claim defended with reasons.

Arguments are composed of one or more premises and a conclusion. **Premises** are statements in an argument offered as evidence or reasons why we should accept another statement, the conclusion. The **conclusion** is the statement in an argument that the premises are intended to prove or support. An argument, accordingly, is a group of statements, one or more of which (called the premises) are intended to prove or support another statement (called the conclusion).

A **statement** is a sentence that can be viewed as either true or false. Here are some examples of statements:

Red is a color.

Canada is in South America.

God does not exist.

Abortion is morally wrong.

Some of these statements are clearly true, some are clearly false, and some are controversial. Each of them is a statement, however, because each can be prefaced with the phrase "It is true that" or "It is false that."

Four things should be noted about statements. First, a sentence may be used to express more than one statement. For example, the grammatical sentence

Roses are red and violets are blue

expresses two distinct statements ("roses are red" and "violets are blue"). Each of these is a statement because each is capable of standing alone as a declarative sentence.

Second, a statement can sometimes be expressed as a phrase or an incomplete clause, rather than as a complete declarative sentence. Consider the sentence

With mortgage interest rates at thirty-year lows, you owe it to yourself to consider refinancing your home. (radio ad)

Grammatically, this is a single declarative sentence. The speaker's intent, however, is clearly to defend one assertion ("You owe it to yourself to consider refinancing your home") on the basis of another ("Mortgage interest rates are at thirty-year lows"). The fact that we have to rephrase the sentence slightly to make this explicit should not obscure the fact that two statements are being offered rather than one.

Third, not all sentences are statements, that is, sentences that either assert or deny that something is the case. Here are some examples of sentences that are not statements:

What time is it? (question)

Hi, Dad! (greeting)

Close the window! (command)

Please send me your current catalog. (request)

Let's go to Paris for our anniversary. (proposal)

Insert tab A into slot B. (instruction)

Oh, my goodness! (exclamation)

None of these is a statement because none of them asserts or denies that anything is the case. None says, in effect, "This is a fact. Accept this; it is true." Consequently, sentences like these are not parts of arguments.

Finally, statements can be about subjective matters of personal experience as well as objectively verifiable matters of fact. If I say, for example,

I feel a slight twinge in my left knee

this is a statement because it is either true or false (I might be lying, after all), even though other people may have no way of verifying whether I am telling the truth.

Not all sentences, however, are as they appear. Some sentences that look like nonstatements are actually statements and can be used in arguments. Here are two examples:

Alyssa, you should quit smoking. Don't you realize how bad that is for your health?

Commencement address: Do not read beauty magazines. They will only make you feel ugly. (Mary Schmich)

The first example contains a rhetorical question. A **rhetorical question** is a sentence that has the grammatical form of a question but is meant to be understood as a statement. In our example, the person asking the question isn't really looking for information. She's making an assertion: that smoking is very bad for one's health. This assertion is offered as a reason (premise) to support the conclusion that Alyssa should quit smoking.

The second example includes an **ought imperative**, that is, a sentence that has the form of an imperative or command but is intended to assert a value or ought judgment about what is good or bad or right or wrong. Grammatically, "Do not read beauty magazines" looks like a command or suggestion. In this context, however, the speaker is clearly making an assertion: that you *shouldn't* read beauty magazines. Her statement that reading such magazines will only make you feel ugly is offered as a reason to support this value judgment.

How can we tell when a sentence that looks like a command or suggestion is really an ought imperative? The key question to ask is this: Can we accurately rephrase the sentence so that it refers to what someone should or ought to do? If we can, the sentence should be regarded as a statement.

Consider two further examples. Suppose a drill sergeant says to a new recruit,

Close that window, soldier! It's freezing in here!

In this context it is clear that the sergeant is issuing an order rather than expressing an ought judgment ("You *ought* to close that window, soldier!"). On the other hand, if one roommate were to say to another,

> Don't blow-dry your hair in the tub, Bert! You could electrocute yourself!

it is likely that the roommate is expressing an ought judgment ("You *shouldn't* blow-dry your hair in the tub!"), rather than issuing an order or making a mere suggestion.

As these examples make clear, it is always important to consider the context in which an expression is used. A sentence such as "Eat your vegetables" might be a command (non-statement) in one context and an ought imperative (statement) in another.

To recap: Imperative sentences are not statements if they are intended as orders, suggestions, proposals, or exhortations. They are statements if they are intended as pieces of advice or value judgments about what someone ought or ought not to do.

Critical Thinking Lapse

A nineteen-year-old man was hospitalized in Salt Lake City after undertaking a personal investigation into the eternal question of whether it is possible to fire a .22-caliber bullet by placing it inside a straw and striking it with a hammer. Answer: Sometimes (including this time); it went off and hit him in the stomach.

Exercise 2.1

I. Determine whether, in typical contexts, the following sentences are or are not statements. Exercises marked with the icon (✪) are answered at the end of the section.

✪ 1. Capital punishment is wrong.

2. Can vegetarians eat animal crackers? (George Carlin)

3. Ted Williams is the greatest hitter in baseball history.

✪ 4. What do you say we stop at the next rest stop?

5. Abraham Lincoln was the first president of the United States.

6. Let's party!

✪ 7. Great!

8. Keep off the grass. (sign)

9. If Sally calls, tell her I'm at the library.

✪ 10. I hope Peter likes his new job.

11. Can't you see that pornography demeans women?

12. Holy cow!

✪ 13. Please print your name legibly.

14. What will it profit a man, if he gains the whole world and forfeits his life?(Matt. 16:2

15. You want mayo on that, right?

✪ 16. What a crock!

17. Give me a call if you have trouble downloading the file.

18. Blondes are more attractive than brunettes.

○19. I'll have a cheeseburger and fries, please, (said to a fast-food restaurant employee)

20. Give us this day our daily bread. (said in prayer)

21. Smoke 'em if you've got 'em.

○22. Mi casa es su casa.

23. Don't you realize how silly that hat looks?

24. What's love but a secondhand emotion? (Tina Turner)

○25. Yikes!

II. Determine whether the following passages do or do not contain ought imperatives.

○ 1. Be nice to your kids. They'll choose your nursing home. (bumper sticker)

2. Toby, never throw a pen at your sister! You could put an eye out! (said by Toby's mother)

3. Never raise your hands to your kids. It leaves your groin unprotected. (George Carlin)

○ 4. If you consume three or more alcoholic drinks every day, ask your doctor whether you should take ibuprofen or other pain relievers/fever reducers. Ibuprofen may cause stomach bleeding, (label)

5. Why don't we eat at El Grande Burrito tonight. I feel like Mexican.

6. If you do not get your first meal service choice, please do not be distressed, as all our entrees taste very much the same. (flight attendant)

○7. Turn off your engine when waiting to pick up the kids. Idling longer than ten seconds in park uses more gas than restarting the car. (Al Gore)

8. In batting practice you must make a point of leaving the bad pitches alone. You don't want your reflexes to get into bad habits. (Mickey Mantle)

9. Don't bother buying premium gas if your car specifies regular. It won't make your car go faster or operate more efficiently—and it's about 14 percent more expensive. (*Consumer Reports* advertising brochure)

○10. Up, sluggard, and waste not life; in the grave will be sleeping enough. (Benjamin Franklin)

11. I never use a whistle in practice. I want the players to get used to reacting to my voice—just like in a real game. (basketball coach Mike Krzyzewski)

12. Associate not with evil men, lest you increase their number. (George Herbert)

○13. If you play [poker] enough, accept that from time to time you are going to go bust, because from time to time, everyone, even the best of the best, does. (Doc Holliday)

14. O Lord, won't you buy me a Mercedes Benz? My friends all drive Porsches; I must make amends. (Janis Joplin)

15. Borrow money from pessimists—they don't expect it back. (Steven Wright)

Identifying Premises and Conclusions

In identifying premises and conclusions, we are often helped by indicator words. **Indicator words** are words or phrases that provide clues that premises or conclusions are being put forward. **Premise indicators** indicate that premises are being offered, and **conclusion indicators** indicate that conclusions are being offered. Here are some common premise indicators:

since	because
for	given that
seeing that	considering that
inasmuch as	as
in view of the fact that	as indicated by
judging from	on account of

The following examples illustrate the use of premise indicators:

Having fun can be the spice of life but not its main course, *because* when it is over, nothing of lasting value remains. (Harold Kushner)

Since effective reasoning requires reliable information, it's important to be able to distinguish good sources and trustworthy experts from less useful ones. (Drew E. Hinderer)

Women are not by any means to blame when they reject the rules of life, which have been introduced into the world, *seeing that* it is men who have made them without their consent. (Michel de Montaigne)

I think that, *as* life is action and passion, it is required of a man that he should share the passion and action of his time, at peril of being judged not to have lived. (Oliver Wendell Holmes Jr.)

And here are some common conclusion indicators:

therefore	thus
hence	consequently
so	accordingly
it follows that	for this reason
that is why	which shows that
wherefore	this implies that
as a result	this suggests that
this being so	we may infer that

These examples illustrate the use of conclusion indicators:

There's probably no God, *so* stop worrying and enjoy your life. (ad on London bus)

Rapid economic improvements represent a life-or-death imperative throughout the Third World. Its people will not be denied that hope, no matter the environmental costs. *As a result*, that choice must not be forced upon them. (Al Gore)

Your life is what your thoughts make it. *That is why* it is important for all of us to guard our minds from unhealthy habits of thinking, habits that hold us back from what we could be accomplishing. (Tom Morris)

As our birth brought us the birth of all things, so will our death bring us the death of all things. *Wherefore* it is as foolish to weep because a hundred years from now we shall not be alive, as to weep because we were not living a hundred years ago. (Michel de Montaigne)

Understanding arguments would be easier if the expressions just listed were used only to signal premises or conclusions. That is not the case, however, as the following examples illustrate:

I haven't seen you *since* high school.

You've had that jacket *for* as long as I've known you.

Thus far everything has been great.

It was *so* cold that even the ski resorts shut down.

I wouldn't mind *seeing that* movie again.

There is water on the floor *because* the sink overflowed.

In none of these examples does the italicized term function as an indicator word. This shows once again why it's so important to consider the context when determining the meaning of an expression.

Many arguments contain no indicator words at all. Here are two examples:

Cats are smarter than dogs. You can't get eight cats to pull a sled through snow. (Jeff Valdez)

I can't be completely responsible for my life. After all, there are many factors outside my control, people and forces that create obstacles and undermine my efforts. And we are subject to pressures and influences from within ourselves: feelings of greed, fear of death, altruistic impulses, sexual compulsions, need for social acceptance, and so on. (John Chaffee, emphasis omitted)

In these passages, there are no indicator words to help us identify the premises and conclusions. Reading carefully, however, we can see that the point of the first passage is to support the claim, "Cats are smarter than dogs," and the point of the second passage is to support the claim, "I can't be completely responsible for my life."

How can we find the conclusion of an argument when the argument contains no indicator words? The following list provides some helpful hints.

Tips on Finding the Conclusion of an Argument

- Find the main issue and ask yourself what position the 'writer or speaker is taking on that issue.

- Look at the beginning or end of the passage; the conclusion is often (but not always) found in one of those places.

- Ask yourself, "What is the writer or speaker trying to prove?" That will be the conclusion.

- Try putting the word *therefore* before one of the statements. If it fits, that statement is probably the conclusion.

- Try the "because" trick. That is, try to find the most appropriate way to fill in the blanks in the following statement: The writer or speaker believes _____ (conclusion) because _____ (premise). The conclusion will naturally come before the word *because*.

Exercise 2.2

I. The following exercises will give you practice in identifying premises and conclusions.

⊙ 1. Since light takes time to reach our eyes, all that we see really existed in the past. (Louis Pojman, *The Theory of Knowledge*)

2. Life changes when you least expect it to. The future is uncertain. So seize this day, seize this moment, and make the most of it. (Jim Valvano, quoted in Mike Krzyzewski, *Leading with the Heart*)

3. Take care of a good name: for this shall continue with thee, more than a thousand treasures precious and great. (*Ecclesiasticus* 41:15)

⊙ 4. I think faith is a vice, because faith means believing a proposition when there is no good reason for believing it. (Bertrand Russell, "The Existence and Nature of God")

> What we have to learn to do we learn by doing.
>
> —Aristotle

5. You want to be very careful about lying; otherwise you are nearly sure to get caught. (Mark Twain, "Advice to Youth")

6. There is no definitive way to prove any one set of religious beliefs to the exclusion of all others. For that reason religious freedom is a human right. (Richard Paul and Linda Elder, *The Miniature Guide to Understanding the Foundations of Ethical Reasoning*)

⊙ 7. Science is based on experiment, on a willingness to challenge old dogma, on an openness to see the universe as it really is. Accordingly, science sometimes requires courage—at the very least the courage to question the conventional wisdom. (Carl Sagan, *Broca's Brain: Reflections on the Romance of Science*)

8. Do not play your sound system loudly as you may not be able to hear warning sirens from emergency vehicles. In addition, hearing damage from loud noise is almost undetectable until it's too late. (car owner's manual)

9. Our attitudes toward creatures that are conscious and capable of experiencing sensations like pain and pleasure are importantly different from our attitudes toward things lacking such capacities, mere chunks of matter or insentient plants, as witness the controversies about vegetarianism and scientific experiments involving live animals. (Jaegwon Kim, *Philosophy of Mind*, 3rd ed.)

⊙ 10. You know how I know animals have souls? Because on average, the lowest animal is a lot nicer and kinder than most of the human beings that inhabit this Earth. (newspaper call-in column)

> We cannot get anywhere without practice.
>
> —Thich Thien-An

11. Democracy has at least one merit, namely, that a member of Parliament cannot be stupider than his constituents, for the more stupid he is, the more stupid they were to elect him. (Bertrand Russell, *Autobiography*)

12. Don't worry about senility. When it hits you, you won't know it. (Bill Cosby, *Time Flies*)

⊙ 13. There is nothing wrong with burning crude [oil] like crazy—oil isn't helping anyone when it sits in the ground—so long as there's a plan for energy alternatives when the cheap oil runs out. (Gregg Easterbrook, "Opportunity Costs")

14. You should always honor your fiercest opponent; the better your opponent, the better you have to be. (Lance Armstrong, *Every Second Counts*)

15. The evil of drunkenness consists partly in the physical deterioration it gradually induces, but far more in the unseating of reason from its ruling position, making the man a temporary beast, and in the disastrous social consequences involved in becoming unfit for any responsible work, such as holding a job or supporting a family. (Austin Fagothey *Right and Reason*, 6th ed.)

16. It's part of human nature to be angry at God when bad things happen, but what's the point? If we encourage each other to blame God for injustices, then aren't we giving the evil or dark side a victory by keeping God's precious children—that's all of us—away from His loving arms? (letter to the editor)

17. In great contests each party claims to act in accordance with the will of God. Both may be, and one must be, wrong. God cannot be for and against the same thing at the same time. (Abraham Lincoln, "Meditation on the Divine Will")

18. There seems to be a tacit assumption that if grizzlies survive in Canada and Alaska, that is good enough. It is not good enough for me. The Alaska bears are a distinct species. Relegating grizzlies to Alaska is about like relegating happiness to heaven; one may never get there. (Aldo Leopold, *A Sand County Almanac*)

19. Has it ever occurred to you how lucky you are to be alive? More than 99 percent of all creatures that have ever lived have died without progeny, but not a single one of your ancestors falls into this group! (Daniel C. Dennett, *Darwin's Dangerous Idea*)

20. Men love the suit so much, we've actually styled our pajamas to look like a tiny suit. Our pajamas have little lapels, little cuffs, simulated breast pockets. Do you need a breast pocket on your pajamas? You put a pen in there, you roll over in the middle of the night, you kill yourself. (Jerry Seinfeld, *SeinLanguage*)

II. Identify the premises and conclusions in the following arguments.

1. When the universe has crushed him man will still be nobler than that which kills him, because he knows that he is dying, and of its victory the universe knows nothing. (Blaise Pascal, *Pensées*)

2. Rights are either God-given or evolve out of the democratic process. Most rights are based on the ability of people to agree on a social contract, the ability to make and keep agreements. Animals cannot possibly reach such an agreement with other creatures. They cannot respect anyone else's rights. Therefore they cannot be said to have rights. (Rush Limbaugh, *The Way Things Ought to Be*)

3. You'd better shape up, 'cuz I need a man, and my heart is set on you. (Olivia Newton-John, *Grease*)

4. Since moral responsibility presupposes free-will, since this freedom is not compatible with universal causal determinism, and since universal causal determinism appears to be the case, it seems evident that—contrary to what most people believe—human beings are not morally responsible, (stated but not endorsed in William H. Halverson, *A Concise Introduction to Philosophy*, 4th ed. [adapted])

5. Our faith comes in moments; our vice is habitual. Yet there is a depth in those brief moments which constrains us to ascribe more reality to them than to all other experiences. For this reason the argument which is always forthcoming to silence those who conceive extraordinary hopes of man, namely the appeal to experience, is forever invalid and vain. (Ralph Waldo Emerson, "The Over-Soul")

6. The travel rule I will stress here is: Never trust anything you read in travel articles. Travel articles appear in publications that sell large, expensive advertisements to tourism-related industries, and these industries do not wish to see articles with headlines like: "URUGUAY: DON'T BOTHER". So no matter what kind of leech-infested, plumbing-free destination travel writers are writing about, they always stress the positive. (Dave Barry, *Dave Barry's Greatest Hits*; emphasis omitted)

7. How can anyone in his right mind criticize the state police for the speed traps? If you're not speeding, you don't have to worry about them. It could save your life if some other speeder is stopped. (newspaper call-in column)

8. Philosophy is dangerous whenever it is taken seriously. But so is life. Safety is not an option. Our choices, then, are not between risk and security, but between a life lived consciously, fully, humanly in the most complete sense and a life that just happens. (Douglas J. Soccio, *Archetypes of Wisdom*, 3rd ed.)

9. Our nation protests, encourages, and even intervenes in the affairs of other nations on the basis of its relations to corporations. But if this is the case, how can we dissociate ourselves from the plight of people in these countries? (Louis P. Pojman, *Global Environmental Ethics*)

✪ 10. If a man say, "I love God," and hateth his brother, he is a liar: for he that loveth not his brother whom he hath seen, how can he love God whom he hath not seen? (I John 4:20)

11. Each of us has an intellectual dimension to his experience. We need ideas as much as we need food, air, or water. Ideas nourish the mind as the latter provide for the body. In light of this, it's clear that we need good ideas as much as we need good food, good air, and good water. (Tom Morris, *If Aristotle Ran General Motors*)

12. What is right in one place may be wrong in another, because the only criterion for distinguishing right from wrong—and so the only ethical standard for judging an action—is the moral system of the society in which the act occurs. (stated but not endorsed in William H. Shaw, *Business Ethics*, 4th ed.)

✪ 13. Whether you like it or not, you'd better accept reality the way it occurs: as highly imperfect and filled with most fallible human beings. Your alternative? Continual anxiety and desperate disappointments. (Albert Ellis and Robert A. Harper, *A New Guide to Rational Living*)

14. We should be emotionally reconciled to the fact of death, rather than fearing it, once we understand that death is necessary for two important, and very positive, things. First, it's necessary for our appreciation of life. The more vivid our sense of the approach of death, the more we relish the small things in life. And secondly, death is necessary for the continued march of evolutionary improvement, an ongoing progress leading to more valuable states of good, to take place on earth. (Tom Morris, *Philosophy for Dummies*)

15. The country life is to be preferred; for there we see the works of God; but in cities little else but the works of man: and the one makes a better object for our contemplation than the other. (William Penn, *Fruits of Solitude*)

✪ 16. Getting in your run early certainly has its advantages. Those who develop the first-thing-in-the-morning routine tend to be more consistent in their training. . . . Morning runs also avoid the heat and peak air pollution. You can enjoy your run without carrying along all the stress that builds up during the day. Early-morning runs . . . save time too by combining your morning and postrun shower. (Bob Glover and Shelly-lynn Florence Glover, *The Competitive Runner's Handbook*)

17. Guys accuse me of constantly singing the praises of Duke [University's men's basketball program]. Well, what is there not to like? You go there and it has everything you dream about in college basketball. Guys play hard. They go to class. They do things the right way. They have discipline. They go out and win. The crowd is behind them. (Dick Vitale, *Campus Chaos*)

18. I wish that someone would give a course in how to live. It can't be taught in the colleges: that's perfectly obvious, for college professors don't know any better than the rest of us. (A. Edward Newton, *The Book-Collecting Game*)

✪ 19. Shop at the farmer's market. You'll begin to eat food in season, when they are at the peak of their nutritional value and flavor, and you'll cook, because you won't find anything processed or microwavable. You'll also be supporting farmers in your community helping defend the countryside from sprawl, saving oil by eating food produced nearby, and teaching your children that a carrot is a root, not a machine-lathed orange bullet that comes in a plastic bag. (Michael Pollan,"Six Reasons for Eating Wisely")

20. The next time you find yourself in an argument, rather than defend your position, see if you can see the other point of view first. . . . When you understand other positions and points of view, several wonderful things begin to happen. First, you often learn something new . . . [and] expand your horizons. Second, when the person you are talking to feels listened to, he or she will appreciate and respect you far more than when you habitually jump in with your own position. . . . A side benefit is that the person you are speaking to may even listen to your point of view. (Richard Carlson, *Don't Sweat the Small Stuff . . . And It's All Small Stuff*)

Critical Thinking Lapse

Larry Walters, a thirty-three-year-old truck driver from North Hollywood, California, had always dreamed about frying. So, on July 2, 1982, Walters tied forty-two Army surplus weather balloons to an aluminum lawn chair, strapped himself in, and cut himself loose.

Walters expected to float lazily over the housetops. Instead, he shot up to 16,000 feet.

Soon Walters found himself drifting into the main approach corridor of Los Angeles International Airport. Shivering with cold, he managed to get himself down by shooting out some balloons with a pellet gun.

Eventually, Walters crashed into some power lines, briefly blacking out a small area in Long Beach.

When asked why he had done it, Walters simply replied, "A man can't just sit around."

What Is Not an Argument?

We encounter arguments everywhere in daily life—at school, at work, in magazine ads, in newspaper editorials, in political discussions, in television documentaries, and on radio talk shows. Of course, people don't use language only to offer arguments: they also use it to tell jokes, sing songs, recite poetry, express feelings, report events, ask questions, offer explanations, say prayers, give orders, and exchange wedding vows. How, then, can we distinguish arguments from nonarguments?

The basic test is quite simple. Something counts as an argument when (1) it is a group of two or more statements and (2) one of those statements (the conclusion) is claimed or intended to be supported by the others (the premises). By applying this simple test, we can usually tell whether a given passage is or is not an argument. Now let's look at five types of nonargumentative discourse that are sometimes confused with arguments:

- reports
- unsupported assertions
- conditional statements
- illustrations
- explanations

Reports

The purpose of a report is simply to convey information about a subject. Here is an example of a report:

Sweeping changes occurred in demographics, economics, culture, and society during the last quarter of the 20th century. The nation aged, and more of its people gravitated to the Sunbelt. Sprawling "urban corridors" and "edge cities" challenged older central cities as sites for commercial, as well as residential, development. Rapid technological change fueled the growth of globalized industries, restructuring the labor force to fit a "postindustrial" economy.

In this passage, the authors are simply reporting a series of events; their aim is to narrate and inform, not to offer reasons why one statement should be accepted on the basis of others.

Caution is needed, however, with reports *about* arguments. Here is an example of such a passage:

Government is legitimate, according to Hobbes, because living under a government is better than living in a state of nature. The advantages of government are so great that it is worth sacrificing some of our freedom in order to bring about these advantages. For this reason, rational people would consent to sign a social contract and subject themselves to the laws and powers of a government.

This is not an argument because the author is merely reporting another person's argument, not endorsing it or putting it forward as his own.

Unsupported Assertions

Unsupported assertions are statements about what a speaker or writer happens to believe. Such statements can be true or false, rational or irrational, but they are parts of arguments only if the speaker or writer claims that they follow from, or support, other claims. Here is an example of a series of unsupported assertions:

> Few may think, yet all have opinions.
> —George Berkeley

I believe that it is not dying that people are afraid of. Something else, something more unsettling and more tragic than dying frightens us. We are afraid of never having lived, of coming to the end of our days with the sense that we were never really alive, that we never figured out what life was for.

Because there is no claim that any of these statements follow from, or imply, any other statements, this is not an argument.

Conditional Statements

A conditional statement is an *if-then* statement. Here are several examples:

If it rains, then the picnic will be canceled.

You must speak French if you grew up in Quebec.

If at first you don't succeed, don't try skydiving.

Conditional statements are made up of two basic parts. The first part, the statement(s) following the word *if*, is called the **antecedent**. The second part, the statement(s) following the word *then*, is called the **consequent**.

Conditional statements need not be explicitly in *if-then* form; in fact, in modern usage, *then* is usually dropped. For example, the following statements are conditional statements:

Should it rain, the picnic will be canceled.

In the event of rain, the picnic will be canceled.

Pete will graduate, provided he passes Critical Thinking.

Conditional statements are not arguments, because there is no claim that any statement *follows* from any part of a conditional statement. Thus, if I say, "If it rains, the picnic will be canceled," I'm not asserting either that it will rain or that the picnic will be canceled.

I'm only asserting that *if* the first statement is true, the second statement will also be true. Because there is no claim that any statement follows from, or supports, this conditional statement, no argument has been given.

Although conditional statements are not arguments, some conditional statements do involve a process of reasoning. Thus, if I say, for example,

> If Rhode Island were larger than Ohio, and Ohio were larger than Texas, then Rhode Island would be larger than Texas

it may appear that I have reasoned to a conclusion, and thus offered an argument. In fact, however, no argument has been given. All I have asserted is that *if* the first two statements are true, then the third statement must also be true. I have not claimed that any of these statements *are* true. Thus, I have not put forward any premises or reasoned to any conclusion. In fact, I have asserted only a single claim: that one statement is true *on the condition* that two other statements are true. Certainly, this claim was arrived at by a process of reasoning, but that does not mean that it is an argument. As we have seen, no single claim by itself is ever an argument.

Conditional statements, accordingly, are not arguments. They can, however, be *parts* of arguments. For example:

> If Sturdley fails Critical Thinking, he'll be placed on academic probation.
>
> Sturdley will fail Critical Thinking.
>
> So, Sturdley will be placed on academic probation.

In fact, arguments can be composed entirely of conditional statements:

> If Tech scores on this play, I'll eat my hat.
>
> If I eat my hat, I'll have a bad case of indigestion.
>
> So, if Tech scores on this play, I'll have a bad case of indigestion.

Such arguments are sometimes called **chain arguments** because the antecedent (the *if* part) of the first statement is linked to the consequent (the *then* part) of the last statement by a chain of intervening conditional statements.

Illustrations

Illustrations are intended to provide examples of a claim, rather than prove or support the claim. Here is an example:

> Many wildflowers are edible. For example, daisies and day lilies are delicious in salads.

Even though the second statement does provide some evidence for the first, this passage is an illustration rather than an argument. Its purpose is not to provide convincing evidence for a conclusion but merely to provide a few notable or representative examples of a claim.

Distinguishing arguments from illustrations can be tricky for two reasons. First, phrases like *for example* and *for instance* sometimes occur in arguments rather than in illustrations. For example:

> *Purists sometimes insist that we should say* between *when two and only two objects are present,* among *if there are more than two. This, however, is an oversimplification. For example, no one would object to* between *in "The main stumbling block in the present delicate exchanges between Paris, Athens, London and Ankara. . . ."*

"For example" is no proof.

—Yiddish proverb

Second, there is sometimes a fine line between illustrating a claim and providing sufficient evidence for the claim. Consider the following:

Many of the world's greatest philosophers were bachelors. For instance, Descartes, Locke, Hume, and Kant were all unmarried.

> Read not to contradict and confute, nor to believe and take for granted . . . but to weigh and consider.
>
> —Francis Bacon

This is a borderline case between an argument and an illustration. Without more information, we cannot tell whether the author's purpose was to provide convincing evidence for a claim or merely to illustrate the claim. Such cases are fairly commonplace and rarely pose any serious difficulty. The general rule here, as with other borderline cases, is simple. Critical thinkers call it *the principle of charity* (see box below).

Applying this simple principle can resolve many otherwise troublesome cases quickly and easily. In the previous example, for instance, it is doubtful whether the four philosophers cited provide sufficient evidence for the claim that "many" of the world's greatest philosophers have been bachelors. It is better, therefore, to treat these as illustrations of the claim rather than as evidence intended to prove the claim.

The Principle of Charity

When interpreting an unclear passage, always give the speaker or writer the benefit of the doubt. Never attribute to an arguer a *weaker* argument when the evidence reasonably permits us to attribute to him or her a *stronger* one. And never interpret a passage as a *bad* argument when the evidence reasonably permits us to interpret it as *not an argument at all*.

Explanations

Consider the following two statements:

Titanic sank because it struck an iceberg.

Capital punishment should be abolished because innocent people may be mistakenly executed.

On the surface, these two statements look very much alike. Both give reasons, and both use the indicator word *because*. There is, however, an important difference between the two: The first statement is an explanation, and the second is an argument.

An **explanation** tries to show *why* something is the case, not to prove *that* it is the case. In the first example, for instance, it is clear that the speaker isn't trying to argue *that Titanic* sank—everybody already knows that it sank. Instead, he is trying to explain *why* it sank. Of course, you can argue about whether a given explanation is or is not correct. Consider this example:

Dinosaurs became extinct because of the impact of a large asteroid.

Scientists argue vigorously about whether this is the correct explanation of the apparently sudden extinction of the dinosaurs sixty-five million years ago. But the fact that this explanation is controversial (i.e., can be argued about) doesn't mean that it is an argument. The purpose of the passage is not to argue *that* dinosaurs became extinct but to explain *why* they became extinct.

Explanations have two parts. The statement that is explained is the **explanandum**. The statement that does the explaining is the **explanans**. Thus, in the explanation

I fell down because I tripped

the statement "I fell down" is the explanandum, and the statement "I tripped" is the explanans.

In everyday speech, we often use "argument" and "explanation" almost interchangeably. Thus, we might say, for example, that the second speaker above is "explaining" why capital punishment should be abolished. This loose way of speaking no doubt contributes greatly to the confusion many students feel in distinguishing arguments from explanations.

Nevertheless, it is important to be able to distinguish arguments from explanations because the standards for evaluating them are quite different. The fact that Schlomo likes mystery stories may be a more or less satisfactory explanation of *why* he is now reading Sir Arthur Conan Doyle's *The Hound of the Baskervilles*, but plainly it is not a good reason for thinking *that* he is now reading that particular book.

How then does one distinguish arguments from explanations? There are four basic tests.

The Common-Knowledge Test First, is the statement that the passage seeks to prove or explain a matter of common knowledge? If it is, the passage is probably an explanation rather than an argument. (There's usually little point in trying to prove something that is already a well-known fact.) Thus, the passage

The North won the American Civil War because it had a larger population and a greater industrial base

is clearly an explanation rather than an argument because it is common knowledge that the North won the Civil War.

The Past-Event Test Second, is the statement that the passage is seeking to prove or explain an event that occurred in the past? If so, the passage is probably an explanation rather than an argument because it is much more common to try to explain *why* past events have occurred rather than to prove *that* they occurred. Thus, the passage

Mel flunked out because he never went to class

is best viewed as an explanation because the speaker is referring to a past event, and we usually try to explain such events rather than provide convincing evidence that they have happened.

The Author's Intent Test Third, is it the speaker's or writer's intent to prove or establish *that* something is the case—that is, *to provide reasons or evidence for accepting a claim as true?* Or is it his intent to explain *why* something is the case—that is, *to offer an account of why some event has occurred or why something is the way it is?* If the former, the passage is an argument; if the latter, the passage is an explanation. Consider this example:

Kevin is majoring in political science because he wants to go to law school.

Here it is unlikely that the speaker is trying to prove that Kevin is majoring in political science, for the "evidence" offered (the fact that Kevin wants to go to law school) would clearly be insufficient to establish that conclusion. It is therefore more likely that the speaker is offering an explanation rather than an argument.

The Principle of Charity Test Fourth, the principle of charity, as we have seen, requires that we always interpret unclear passages generously and, in particular, that we never interpret a passage as a bad argument when the evidence reasonably permits us to interpret it as not an argument at all. This test often proves helpful when the other tests yield no clear answer. For example:

Jeremy won't come to the frat party tonight because he has an important exam tomorrow.

This claim about Jeremy is not common knowledge, nor does it refer to a past event. Thus, neither the common-knowledge test nor the past-event test is applicable to this example. The third test—the author's intent test—also yields no clear answer; the speaker might reasonably be interpreted as offering either an argument or an explanation. If we interpret the passage as an argument, however, the reasoning is bound to strike us as somewhat weak. Our choice therefore (assuming that a choice must be made) is to interpret the passage either as a weak argument or as an apparently satisfactory explanation. In these circumstances the principle of charity dictates that we interpret the passage as an explanation.

It should be noted that none of these four tests is foolproof. Consider this example:

All men are mortal, and Socrates is a man. Therefore, Socrates is mortal.

Here the concluding statement ("Socrates is mortal") is a matter of common knowledge. Generally, as we have noted, we don't argue for conclusions that are well-known matters of fact; yet, clearly, the passage is an argument. The past-event test also has exceptions, as this example illustrates:

No single shooter could have shot as quickly and as accurately as Lee Harvey Oswald is alleged to have done in the Kennedy assassination. Therefore, Oswald was not the lone assassin.

The statement this passage seeks to prove or explain is about an event that occurred in the past, yet clearly the passage is an argument.

Sometimes none of the four tests yields a clear answer. In real life, of course, passages don't come neatly labeled as "argument" or "explanation." And the truth is that sometimes we just can't tell whether a passage is meant to be an argument or an explanation. Consider this quote from former ACLU president Nadine Strossen:

Because civil libertarians have learned that free speech is an indispensable instrument for the promotion of other rights and freedoms—including racial equality—we fear that the movement to regulate campus expression will undermine equality, as well as free speech.

What is the author's intent here? Is she trying to *explain* why civil libertarians fear that campus speech codes may undermine both freedom and equality? Or is she offering a *reason* why everyone should be concerned about such possible consequences? Or is she perhaps doing both? It is very difficult to say, and none of our four tests yields a clear answer.

Some students find it frustrating that critical thinking doesn't always provide definite, clear-cut answers. In this respect, however, critical thinking simply reflects life. Life is complex and messy, and critical thinking, because it helps us think intelligently about life, naturally reflects this complexity and messiness. Sometimes despite our best efforts we can't be sure whether a passage is an argument or an explanation. When that happens, we shouldn't pretend that a passage is clear. Instead, we should look at the various possibilities and say, "Well, it's unclear whether this is an argument or an explanation.

However, if it's an argument, it is a good [bad] argument because —————————. And if it's an explanation, it is a good [bad] explanation because————————." It is often possible to evaluate a passage in this way, even if we can't be sure how the passage should be understood.

Exercise 2.3

Arrange the chairs in the class into a circle. The instructor will give each student a 3 X 5 index card. On one side of the card, write a very brief example of either an argument or an explanation. On the other side of the card, write "argument" or "explanation," whichever is appropriate to your example. When everyone has finished writing, pass your card to the student sitting to your right. Read the card you have received and decide whether it is an argument or an explanation, then check your answer with the answer indicated on the back. Continue passing the cards until each card has been read. The instructor will then collect the cards and discuss the examples with the class.

Exercise 2.4

I. Determine which of the following passages contain arguments and which do not.

◐ 1. I ate because I was hungry.

2. He must be home. His car's in the driveway.

3. I'm trading in my Ford Explorer for a Toyota Corolla because they're more reliable and get better gas mileage.

◐ 4. If Christmas is on a Friday, the day after Christmas must be a Saturday.

5. Dinosaurs became extinct sixty-five million years ago, probably as a result of dramatic global cooling that resulted from the impact of a large asteroid.

6. Dogs make better pets than cats because they're more intelligent and obedient.

◐ 7. According to baseball statistician Bill James, Stan Musial was a better all-around baseball player than Ted Williams because Musial was, in addition to being a great hitter, a better fielder and base-runner than Williams was.

8. The rich and famous tend not to be happy, well-adjusted personalities. Look at Britney Spears.

9. I stayed home from school because I was sick.

◐ 10. The Cascades mountain range contains many majestic peaks. Mt. Rainier and Mt. Hood, for instance, are both more than ten thousand feet.

11. Animals have a prodigious advantage over us: they forsee neither evils nor death. (Voltaire, *Notebooks*)

12. If there were no maldistribution, if everyone shared equally, and if no grain were fed to animals, all of humanity could be adequately nourished today. (Paul Ehrlich and Anne Ehrlich, *Betrayal of Science and Reason*)

◐ 13. The British statesman William Gladstone thought that we would all be healthier if we chewed each bite of food precisely 32 times. Why else, he argued, did nature endow us with exactly 32 teeth? (Thomas Gilovich, *How We Know What Isn't So*)

14. Guys are extremely reluctant to make commitments, or even to take any steps that might lead to commitments. That is why, when a guy goes out on a date with a woman and finds himself really liking her, he often will demonstrate his affection by avoiding her for the rest of his life. (Dave Barry, *Dave Barry's Complete Guide to Guys*)

15. You can fool all of the people some of the time, and some of the people all the time, but you cannot fool all the people all the time. (Abraham Lincoln)

◐ 16. A new study published in the journal *Pediatrics* found that removing a child's tonsils and adenoids can lead to better grades, presumably because the surgery allows for a better night's sleep. (Stacey Burling, "Tonsillectomy Can Hike Grades, New Study Says")

17. Productivity and serving the public and taking care of one's own employees are neither mere means nor an afterthought of business but rather its very essence. Then, as every smart entrepreneur knows well enough, the profits will come as a consequence. (Robert C. Solomon, *Ethics and Excellence: Cooperation and Integrity in Business*)

18. It is clear that there never was a time when nothing existed; otherwise nothing would exist now. (C. S. Lewis, *Miracles*)

✪ 19. Children should be taught not to steal because it is wrong. They should not be taught not to steal because there is a rule against stealing. (J. F. Covaleski, "Discipline and Morality: Beyond Rules and Consequences")

20. The wind blows where it wills, and you hear the sound of it, but you do not know whence it comes or whither it goes; so it is with every one who is born of the Spirit. (John 3:8)

21. However "civilized," however much brought up in an artificially contrived environment, we all seem to have an innate longing for primitive simplicity, close to the natural state of living. Hence the city people's pleasure in the summer camping in the woods or traveling in the desert or opening up an unbeaten track. (D.T. Suzuki, *Zen and Japanese Culture*)

✪ 22. More than any other time in history, mankind faces a crossroads. One path leads to despair and utter hopelessness, the other, to total extinction. Let us pray that we have the wisdom to choose correctly. (Woody Allen, *Side Effects*)

23. What's right in the corporation is not what is right in a man's home or in his church. What is right in the corporation is what the guy above you wants from you. That's what morality is in the corporation. (Robert Jackal, *Moral Mazes*)

24. Never hit your child. Today health professionals agree that hitting children harms them emotionally as well as physically, fosters rage and self-hate, and often does lasting damage to their self-esteem and sense of worth. (Dr. C. Everett Koop, *Dr. Koop's Self-Help Advisor*)

✪ 25. Tradition and folklore contain a large number of fallacious beliefs. For example, many widespread and popular beliefs such as "Don't swim for an hour after eating," "You should rub snow on frost bite," "Reading in the dark will ruin your eyes," "You can catch cold from being chilled," and "The more you cut your hair, the faster it will grow" are not true. (I.W. Kelly et al, "The Moon Was Full and Nothing Happened: A Review of Studies on the Moon and Human Behavior and Human Belief")

26. If you don't listen to radio talk shows, you really should, because it gives you a chance to reassure yourself that a great many people out there are much stupider than you are. (Dave Barry, *Dave Barry's Bad Habits*)

27. I don't want to achieve immortality through my works. I want to achieve immortality through not dying. (Woody Allen)

✪ 28. When what is just or unjust is thought to be determined solely by whoever has the power to lay down the law of the land, it unavoidably follows that the lay of the land cannot be judged either just or unjust. (Mortimer J. Adler, *Six Great Ideas*)

29. Observe that noses were made to wear spectacles, and so we have spectacles. (Voltaire, *Candide*)

30. Your manuscript is both good and original; but the part that is good is not original, and the part that is original is not good. (Samuel Johnson)

II. Determine whether the following passages are best understood as arguments or explanations.

✪ 1. Neptune is blue because its atmosphere contains methane. (John Fix, *Astronomy: Journey to the Cosmic Frontier*, 2nd ed.)

2. A good schoolmaster is a far more useful citizen than the average bank president, politician, or general, if only because what he transmits is what gives meaning to the life of the banker, the politician, the general. (Clifton Fadiman, *The Lifetime Reading Plan*)

3. My mother, who graduated from high school at sixteen, had no hope of affording college, so she went to work in the local post office for a dollar a day. (Tom Brokaw, *The Greatest Generation*)

○ 4. Since rights claimed against the government should (at least within a democracy) be held equally by all citizens, and since not every citizen could be employed by the government, citizens cannot claim a right to a job from the government. (Joseph Desjardins, *An Introduction to Business Ethics*)

5. Why are there laws of gravity? Because, Einstein revealed, large masses distort space-time, causing objects to move along geodesic paths. (Martin Gardner, "Science and the Unknowable")

6. The Great Lakes area has a concentration of industry because of the availability of water for manufacturing processes, and because water transportation is an efficient way to move raw materials and products. (Eldon E. Enger and Bradley E Smith, *Environmental Science*, 6th ed.)

○ 7. True success always starts with an inner vision, however incomplete it might be. That's why most of the books on success by famous coaches, business stars, motivational consultants, and psychologists begin with chapters on goal setting. (Tom Morris, *Philosophy for Dummies*)

8. It is a fact of life on our beleaguered little planet that widespread torture, famine, and governmental criminal irresponsibility are much more likely to be found in tyrannous than in democratic governments. Why? Because the rulers of the former are much less likely to be thrown out of office for their misdeeds than the rulers of the latter. (Carl Sagan, *The Demon-Haunted World: Science as a Candle in the Dark*)

9. Men seem to fly around the television more than women. Men get that remote control in their hands, they don't even know what the hell they're not watching. . . . Women don't do this. Women will stop and go, "Well let me see what the show is, before I change the channel. Maybe we can nurture it, work with it, help it grow into something." Men don't do that. Because women nest and men hunt. That's why we watch TV differently. (Jerry Seinfeld, *SeinLanguage*)

○ 10. A bullet has no conscience; neither does a malignant tumor or an automobile gone out of control. This is why good people get sick and get hurt as much as anyone. (Harold Kushner, *When Bad Things Happen to Good People*)

11. We are bound to run into trouble if we seek rational justifications of every principle we use, for one cannot provide a rational argument for rational argument itself without assuming what we are arguing for. (A. F. Chalmers, *What Is This Thing Called Science?* 3rd ed.)

12. Most of us find the ideal of promoting human happiness and well-being an attractive one and, as a result, admire greatly people like Mother Teresa (1910–1997), who devoted her life to working with the poor. (William H. Shaw, *Business Ethics*, 4th ed.)

○ 13. Good hitters have good work habits. They know that practice and lots of it is the surest way to eliminate slumps. And they know that practice is essential to maintaining their edge. Consequently, good hitters are usually always working on something. (Charley Lau, *The Art of Hitting .300*)

14. I always turn to the sports section first. The sports page records people's accomplishments; the front page has nothing but man's failures. (Earl Warren, quoted in Steve Rushin, "The Season of High Heat")

15. Men may live more truly and fully in reading Plato and Shakespeare than at any other time, because then they are participating in essential being and are forgetting their accidental lives. (Allan Bloom, *The Closing of the American Mind*)

○ 16. Because height is inherited, short people bear shorter children than tall people on average. (Wendy Northcutt, *The Darwin Awards*)

17. I don't think in our society when we spend $3 billion on pets, that there's any reason for a child to starve to death. (Robert F. Kennedy, speech)

18. I wear glasses primarily so I can look for the things that I keep losing. (Bill Cosby, *Time Flies*)

o 19. [NBA] superstars with dramatic, eye-catching moves are paid vast sums of money while players who contribute to the team effort in less flamboyant ways often make close to the minimum salary. As a result, few players come to the NBA dreaming of becoming good team players. (Phil Jackson and Hugh Delehanty *Sacred Hoops: Spiritual Lessons of a Hardwood Warrior*)

20. I come from the Lower East Side of New York City and from very rough circumstances. As a matter of fact, I came from a family of fourteen children. Fourteen children. It's true. It happened because my mother was hard of hearing. I'll explain this to you. You see, every night when it was time to retire, my father would turn to my mother and say, "Would you like to go to sleep or what?" My mother, who couldn't hear very well would say, "What?" And that's how it happened. (Jackie Mason, *Jackie Mason's America*)

Summary

1. Because critical thinking is concerned primarily with understanding, constructing, and critically evaluating arguments, one of the most basic critical thinking skills is that of recognizing arguments.

2. An *argument,* as that term is used in critical thinking, is a claim defended with reasons. Arguments are composed of one or more premises and a conclusion. *Premises* are statements in an argument offered as evidence or reasons in support of another statement. A *statement* is a sentence that can be viewed as either true or false. A *conclusion* is the statement in an argument that the premises are intended to support or prove.

3. *Indicator words* provide clues that premises or conclusions are being offered. Common indicator words include *therefore, consequently, thus, because,* and *since. Premise indicators* provide clues that premises are being offered, and *conclusion indicators* provide clues that conclusions are being offered. Indicator words, however, should be approached with caution because not all arguments contain indicator words, and sometimes indicator words are used in passages that are not arguments.

4. It is important to distinguish arguments from various kinds of nonargumentative discourse, such as reports, unsupported assertions, conditional statements, illustrations, and explanations. *Reports* are statements that are intended simply to convey information about a subject. *Unsupported assertions* are statements that indicate what a person believes but don't offer evidence for that belief. *Conditional statements* are *if-then* statements. They claim only that one statement is true *if* another statement is true. *Illustrations* are statements intended to provide examples of a claim, rather than evidence or proof for the claim. *Explanations* are statements intended to explain *why* something is the case, rather than to prove *that* it is the case. None of these types of passages is an argument because none is intended to prove a claim.

Answers to Selected Exercises

Exercise 2.1

I.

1. Statement.
4. Nonstatement; suggestion.
7. Statement. (This is a brief and emphatic way of saying "This is great.")

10. Statement. (You might be lying.)
13. Nonstatement; request.
16. Statement. (This is an emphatic way of saying "This is a crock.")
19. Nonstatement; request.
22. Statement. (Spanish for "My house is your house.")
25. Nonstatement; exclamation.

II.

1. Yes.
4. Yes.
7. Yes.
10. Yes.
13. Yes.

Exercise 2.2

I.

1. *Premise:* Light takes time to reach our eyes.
   Conclusion: All that we see really existed in the past.
4. *Premise:* Faith means believing a proposition when there is no good reason for believing it.
   Conclusion: Faith is a vice.
7. *Premise:* Science is based on experiment, on a willingness to see the universe as it really is.
   Conclusion: Science sometimes requires courage—at the very least the courage to question the conventional wisdom.
10. *Premise:* The lowest animal is a lot nicer and kinder than most of the humans beings that inhabit this earth. *Conclusion:* Animals have souls.
13. *Premise:* Oil isn't helping anyone when it sits in the ground.
    Conclusion: There is nothing wrong with burning crude oil like crazy—so long as there's a plan for energy alternatives when the cheap oil runs out.
16. *Premise:* If we encourage each other to blame God for injustices, we are giving the evil or dark side a victory by keeping God's precious children—that's all of us—away from His loving arms.
    Conclusion: Although it is part of human nature to be angry at God when bad things happen, there is no point in doing so.
19. *Premise 1:* More than 99 percent of all the creatures that have ever lived have died without progeny.
    Premise 2: Not a single one of your ancestors falls into this group.
    Conclusion: You are lucky to be alive.

II.

1. *Premise 1:* Man knows that he is dying.
   Premise 2: Of its victory over man, the universe knows nothing.
   Conclusion: When the universe has crushed him, man will be nobler than that which kills him.
4. *Premise 1:* Moral responsibility presupposes freewill.
   Premise 2: This freedom is not compatible with universal causal determination. *Premise 3:* Universal causal determinism appears to be the case.
   Conclusion: Contrary to what most people believe, human beings are not morally responsible.
7. *Premise 1:* If you're not speeding, you don't have to worry about speed traps.
   Premise 2: A speed trap could save your life if some other speeder is stopped.
   Conclusion: No one in his right mind should criticize the state police for the speed traps.
10. *Premise:* He that loveth not his brother whom he hath seen, cannot love God whom he hath not seen.
    Conclusion: If a man say, "I love God," and hateth his brother, he is a liar.

13. *Premise:* Your alternative to accepting reality the way it occurs is continuous anxiety and desperate disappointments.
Conclusion: Whether you like it or not, you'd better accept reality the way it occurs: as highly imperfect and filled with the most fallible human beings.

16. *Premise 1:* Those who develop the first-thing-in-the-morning routine tend to be more consistent in their training.
Premise 2: Morning runs avoid the heat and peak air pollution.
Premise 3: You can enjoy your runs without carrying along all the stress that builds up during the day.
Premise 4: Early-morning runs save time by combining your morning and postrun shower.
Conclusion: Getting in your run early certainly has its advantages.

19. *Premise 1:* You'll begin to eat food in season, when it is at the peak of its nutritional value and flavor.
Premise 2: You won't find anything processed or microwavable.
Premise 3 (subconclusion): You'll cook.
Premise 4: You'll be supporting the farmers in your community.
Premise 5: You'll be helping defend the countryside from sprawl.
Premise 6: You'll be saving oil by eating food produced nearby.
Premise 7: You'll be teaching your children that a carrot is a root, not a machine-lathed orange bullet that comes in a plastic bag.
Conclusion: Shop at the farmer's market.

Exercise 2.4

I.

1. Nonargument; explanation.
4. Nonargument; conditional statement.
7. Nonargument; report of an argument.
10. Nonargument; illustration.
13. Nonargument; report of an argument.
16. Nonargument, report of an explanation.
19. Nonargument; unsupported assertion. (Notice that the word *because* does not function as a premise indicator in either sentence of this passage.)
22. Nonargument. (No conclusion is drawn.)
25. Nonargument; illustration.
28. Nonargument; conditional statement. (*When* here means "if.")

II.

1. Explanation.
4. Argument.
7. Explanation.
10. Explanation.
13. Explanation.
16. Explanation.
19. Explanation.

from **Thinking Critically**

John Chaffe

Understanding Deductive Arguments

We use a number of basic argument forms to organize, relate to, and make sense of the world. . . . [T]wo of the major types of argument forms are **deductive arguments** and *inductive arguments*. In the remainder of this chapter, we will explore various types of deductive arguments, reserving our analysis of inductive arguments . . .

The deductive argument is the one most commonly associated with the study of logic.

Deductive Argument

An argument form in which one reasons from premises that are known or assumed to be true to a conclusion that follows necessarily from these premises

Though it has a variety of valid forms, they all share one characteristic: If you accept the supporting reasons (also called *premises*) as true, then you must necessarily accept the conclusion as true.

For example, consider the following famous deductive argument:

REASON/PREMISE: All men are mortal.

REASON/PREMISE: Socrates is a man.

CONCLUSION: Therefore, Socrates is mortal.

In this example of deductive thinking, accepting the premises of the argument as true means that the conclusion necessarily follows; it cannot be false. Many deductive arguments, like the one just given, are structured as *syllogisms*, an argument form that consists of two supporting premises and a conclusion. There are also, however, a large number of *invalid* deductive forms, one of which is illustrated in the following syllogism:

REASON/PREMISE: All men are mortal.

REASON/PREMISE: Socrates is a man.

CONCLUSION: Therefore, all men are Socrates.

In the next several pages, we will briefly examine some common valid deductive forms.

Application of a General Rule

Whenever we reason with the form illustrated by the valid Socrates syllogism, are using the following argument structure:

PREMISE: All *A* (men) are *B* (mortal).

PREMISE: *S* is an *A* (Socrates is a man).

CONCLUSION: Therefore, *S* is *B* (Socrates is mortal).

This basic argument form is valid no matter what terms are included. For example:

PREMISE: All politicians are untrustworthy.

PREMISE: Bill White is a politician.

CONCLUSION: Therefore, Bill White is untrustworthy.

Notice again that with any valid deductive form, *if* we assume that the premises are true, then we must accept the conclusion. Of course, in this case there is considerable doubt that the first premise is actually true.

When we diagram this argument form, it becomes clear why it is a valid way thinking:

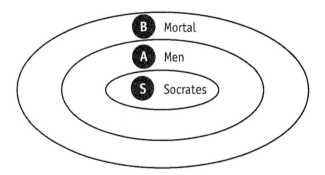

The *first premise* states that classification *A* (men) falls within classification *B* (mortal).

The *second premise* states that *S* (Socrates) is a member of classification *A* (men).

The *conclusion* simply states what has now become obvious—namely, that *S* (Socrates) must fall within classification *B* (mortal).

Although we are usually not aware of it, we use this basic type of reasoning whenever we apply a general rule in the form *All A is B*. For instance:

PREMISE: All children eight years old should be in bed by 9:30 P.M.

PREMISE: You are an eight-year-old child.

CONCLUSION: Therefore, you should be in bed by 9:30 P.M.

• • •

[*ed.*: Can you think of an example from your own experience in which you use this deductive form?]

Modus Ponens

A second valid deductive form that we commonly use in our thirddng goes by the name *modus ponens*—that is, "affirming the antecedent"—and is illustrated in the following example:

PREMISE: If I have prepared thoroughly for the final exam, then I will do well.

PREMISE: I prepared thoroughly for the exam.

CONCLUSION: Therefore, I will do well on the exam.

When we reason like this, we are using the following argument structure:

PREMISE: If *A* (I have prepared thoroughly), then *B* (I will do well).

PREMISE: *A* (I have prepared thoroughly).

CONCLUSION: Therefore, *B* (I will do well).

Like all valid deductive forms, this form is valid no matter what specific terms are included. For example:

PREMISE: If the Democrats are able to register 20 million new voters, then they will win the presidential election.

PREMISE: The Democrats were able to register more than 20 million new voters.

CONCLUSION: Therefore, the Democrats will win the presidential election.

As with other valid argument forms, the conclusion will be true *if* the reasons are true. Although the second premise in this argument expresses information that can be verified, the first premise would be more difficult to establish. . . .

[*ed.*: Can you think of an example from your own experience in which you use this deductive form?]

Modus Tollens

A third commonly used valid deductive form has the name *modus tollens*—that is, "denying the consequence"—and is illustrated in the following example:

PREMISE: If Michael were a really good friend, he would lend me his car for the weekend.

PREMISE: Michael refuses to lend me his car for the weekend.

CONCLUSION: Therefore, Michael is not a really good friend.

When we reason in this fashion, we are using the following argument structure:

PREMISE: If *A* (Michael is a really good friend), then *B* (he will lend me his car).

PREMISE: Not *B* (he won't lend me his car).

CONCLUSION: Therefore, not *A* (he's not a really good friend).

Again, like other valid reasoning forms, this form is valid no matter what subject is being considered. For instance:

PREMISE: If Iraq were genuinely interested in world peace, it would not have invaded Kuwait.

PREMISE: Iraq did invade Kuwait (that is, Iraq did not "not invade" Kuwait).

CONCLUSION: Therefore, Iraq is not genuinely interested in world peace.

This conclusion—and any other conclusion produced by this form of reasoning—can be considered accurate if the reasons are true. In this case, the second premise would be easier to verify than the first. . . .

[*ed*.: Can you think of an example from your own experience in which you use this deductive form?]

Disjunctive Syllogism

A fourth common form of a valid deductive argument is known as a *disjunctive syllogism*. The term *disjunctive* means presenting several alternatives. This form is illustrated in the following example:

PREMISE: Either I left my wallet on my dresser, or I have lost it.

PREMISE: The wallet is not on my dresser.

CONCLUSION: Therefore, I must have lost it.

When we reason in this way, we are using the following argument structure:

PREMISE: Either *A* (I left my wallet on my dresser) or *B* (I have lost it).

PREMISE: Not *A* (I didn't leave it on my dresser).

CONCLUSION: Therefore, *B* (I have lost it).

This valid reasoning form can be applied to any number of situations and still yield valid results. For example:

PREMISE: Either your stomach trouble is caused by what you are eating, or it is caused by nervous tension.

PREMISE: You tell me that you have been taking special care with your diet.

CONCLUSION: Therefore, your stomach trouble is caused by nervous tension.

To determine the accuracy of the conclusion, we must determine the accuracy of the premises. If they are true, then the conclusion must be true. . . .

[*ed*.: Can you think of an example from your own experience in which you use this deductive form?]

All these basic argument forms—application of a general rule, *modus ponens, modus tollens,* and disjunctive syllogism—are found not only in informal, everyday conversations but also at more formal levels of thinking. They appear in academic disciplines, in scientific inquiry, in debates on social issues, and elsewhere. Many other argument forms—both deductive and inductive—also constitute human reasoning. By sharpening your understanding of these ways of thinking, you will be better able to make sense of the world by constructing and evaluating effective arguments.

Thinking Activity

EVALUATING ARGUMENTS

Analyze the following arguments by completing these steps:

1. Summarize the reasons and conclusions given.
2. Identify which, if any, of the following deductive argument forms are used.

- Application of a general rule
- *Modus ponens* (affirming the antecedent)
- *Modus tollens* (denying the consequence)
- Disjunctive syllogism

3. Evaluate the truth of the reasons that support the conclusion.

For if the brain is a machine of ten billion nerve cells and the mind can somehow be explained as the summed activity of a finite number of chemical and electrical reactions, [then] boundaries limit the human prospect—we are biological and our souls cannot fly free.

—Edward O. Wilson, *On Human Nature*

The state is by nature clearly prior to the family and to the individual, since the whole is of necessity prior to the part.

—Aristotle, *Politics*

There now is sophisticated research that strongly suggests a deterrent effect [of capital punishment]. Furthermore, the principal argument against the deterrent effect is weak. The argument is that in most jurisdictions where capital punishment has been abolished there has been no immediate, sharp increase in what had been capital crimes. But in those jurisdictions, the actual act of abolition was an insignificant event because for years the death penalty had been imposed rarely, if at all. Common sense—which deserves deference until it is refuted— suggests that the fear of death can deter some premeditated crimes, including some murders.

—George F. Will, *Cleveland Plain-Dealer*, March 13, 1981

If the increased power which science has conferred upon human volitions is to be a boon and not a curse, the ends to which these volitions are directed must grow commensurately with the growth of power to carry them out. Hitherto, although we have been told on Sundays to love our neighbor, we have been told on weekdays to hate him, and there are six times as many weekdays as Sundays. Hitherto, the harm that we could do to our neighbor by hating him was limited by our incompetence, but in the new world upon which we are entering there will be no such limit, and the indulgence of hatred can lead only to ultimate and complete disaster.

—Bertrand Russell, "The Expanding Mental Universe"

The extreme vulnerability of a complex industrial society to intelligent, targeted terrorism by a very small number of people may prove the fatal challenge to which Western states have no adequate response. Counterforce alone will never suffice. The real challenge of the true terrorist is to the basic values of a society. If there is no commitment to shared values in Western society—and if none are imparted in our amoral institutions of higher learning—no increase in police and burglar alarms will suffice to preserve our society from the specter that haunts us—not a bomb from above but a gun from within.

—James Billington, "The Gun Within"

To fully believe in something, to truly understand something, one must be intimately acquainted with its opposite. One should not adopt a creed by default, because no alternative is known. Education should prepare students for the "real world" not by segregating them from evil but by urging full confrontation to test and modify the validity of the good.

—Robert Baron, "In Defense of 'Teaching' Racism, Sexism, and Fascism"

The inescapable conclusion is that society secretly wants crime, needs crime, and gains definite satisfactions from the present mishandling of it! We condemn crime; we punish offenders for it; but we need it. The crime and punishment ritual is a part of our lives. We need crimes to wonder at, to enjoy vicariously, to discuss and speculate about, and to publicly deplore. We need criminals to identify ourselves with, to envy secretly, and to punish stoutly. They do for us the forbidden, illegal things we wish to do and, like scapegoats of old, they bear the burdens of our displaced guilt and punishment—"the iniquities of us all."

—Karl Menninger, "The Crime of Punishment"

Inductive Reasoning

Inductive Reasoning

An argument form in which one reasons from premises that are known or assumed to be true to a conclusion that is supported by the premises but does not necessarily follow from them.

When you reason inductively, your premises provide evidence that makes it more or less probable (but not certain) that the conclusion is true. The following statements are examples of conclusions reached through inductive reasoning.

1. A recent Gallup Poll reported that 74 percent of the American public believes that abortion should remain legalized.

2. On the average, a person with a college degree will earn over $1,140,000 more in his or her lifetime than a person with just a high-school diploma.

3. In a recent survey twice as many doctors interviewed stated that if they were stranded on a desert island, they would prefer Bayer Aspirin to Extra Strength Tylenol.

4. The outbreak of food poisoning at the end-of-year school party was probably caused by the squid salad.

5. The devastating disease AIDS is caused by a particularly complex virus that may not be curable.

6. The solar system is probably the result of an enormous explosion—a "big bang"—that occurred billions of years ago.

The first three statements are forms of inductive reasoning known as *empirical generalization,* a general statement about an entire group made on the basis of observing some members of the group. The final three statements are examples of *causal reasoning,* a form of inductive reasoning in which it is claimed that an event (or events) is the result of the occurrence of another event (or events). We will be exploring the ways each of these forms of inductive reasoning functions in our lives and in various fields of study.

Empirical Generalization

One of the most important tools used by both natural and social scientists is empirical generalization. Have you ever wondered how the major television and radio networks can accurately predict election results hours before the polls close? These predictions are made possible by the power of **empirical generalization**, a first major type of inductive reasoning that is defined as reasoning from a limited sample to a general conclusion based on this sample.

Empirical Generalization

A form of inductive reasoning in which a general statement is made about an entire group (the "target population") based on observing some members of the group (the "sample population")

Network election predictions, as well as public opinion polls that occur throughout a political campaign, are based on interviews with a select number of people. Ideally, pollsters would interview everyone in the *target population* (in this case, voters), but this, of course, is hardly practical. Instead, they select a relatively small group of individuals from the target population, known as a *sample*, who they have determined will adequately represent the group as a whole. Pollsters believe that they can then generalize the opinions of this smaller group to the target population. And with a few notable exceptions (such as in the 1948 presidential election, when New York governor Thomas Dewey went to bed believing he had been elected president and woke up a loser to Harry Truman, and the 2000 election, when Al Gore was briefly declared the presidential winner over George W. Bush), these results are highly accurate.

There are three key criteria for evaluating inductive arguments:

- Is the sample known?
- Is the sample sufficient?
- Is the sample representative?

Is the Sample Known?

An inductive argument is only as strong as the sample on which it is based. For example, sample populations described in vague and unclear terms—"highly placed sources" or "many young people interviewed," for example—provide a treacherously weak foundation for generalizing to larger populations. In order for an inductive argument to be persuasive, the sample population should be explicitly known and clearly identified. Natural and social scientists take great care in selecting the members in the sample groups, and this is an important part of the data that is available to outside investigators who may wish to evaluate and verify the results.

Is the Sample Sufficient?

The second criterion for evaluating inductive reasoning is to consider the size of the sample. It should be sufficiently large enough to give an accurate sense of the group as a whole. In the polling example discussed earlier, we would be concerned if only a few registered voters had been interviewed, and the results of these interviews were then generalized to a much larger population. Overall, the larger the sample, the more reliable the inductive conclusions. Natural and social scientists have developed precise guidelines for determining the size of the sample needed to achieve reliable results. For example, poll results are often accompanied by a qualification such as "These results are subject to an error factor of ±3 percentage points." This means that if the sample reveals that 47 percent of those interviewed prefer candidate X, then we can reliably state that 44 to 50 percent of the target population prefer candidate X. Because a sample is usually a small portion of the target population, we can rarely state that the two match each other exactly—there must always be some room for variation. The exceptions to this are situations in which the target population is completely homogeneous. For example, tasting one cookie from a bag of cookies is usually enough to tell us whether or not the entire bag is stale.

The third crucial element in effective inductive reasoning is the *representativeness* of the sample. If we are to generalize with confidence from the sample to the target population, then we have to be sure the sample is similar to the larger group from which it is drawn in all relevant aspects. For instance, in the polling example the sample population should reflect the same percentage of men and women, of Democrats and Republicans, of young and old, and so on, as the target population. It is obvious that many characteristics, such as hair color, favorite food, and shoe size, are not relevant to the comparison. The better the sample reflects the target population in terms of *relevant* qualities, the better the accuracy of the generalizations. However, when the sample is *not* representative of the target population— for example, if the election pollsters interviewed only females between the ages of thirty and thirty-five—then the sample is termed *biased*, and any generalizations about the target population will be highly suspect.

How do we ensure that the sample is representative of the target population? One important device is *random selection*, a selection strategy in which every member of the target population has an equal chance of being included in the sample. For example, the various techniques used to select winning lottery tickets are supposed to be random—each ticket is supposed to have an equal chance of winning. In complex cases of inductive reasoning— such as polling—random selection is often combined with the confirmation that all of the important categories in the population are adequately represented. For example, an election pollster would want to be certain that all significant geographical areas are included and then would randomly select individuals from within those areas to compose the sample.

Understanding the principles of empirical generalization is of crucial importance to effective thinking because we are continually challenged to construct and evaluate this form of inductive argument in our lives. . . .

Thinking Activity

DESIGNING A POLL

Select an issue that you would like to poll a group of people about—for example, the population of your school or your neighborhood. Describe in specific terms how you would go about constructing a sample both large and representative enough for you to generalize the results to the target population accurately.

Causal Reasoning

A second major type of inductive reasoning is **causal reasoning,** a form in which an event (or events) is claimed to be the result of the occurrence of another event (or events).

> ## *Causal Reasoning*
> A form of inductive reasoning in which an event (or events) is claimed to be the result of another event (or events)

As you use your thinking abilities to try to understand the world you live in, you often ask the question "Why did that happen?" For example, if the engine of your car is running roughly, your natural question is "What's wrong?" If you wake up one morning with an upset stomach, you usually ask yourself, "What's the cause?" Or maybe the softball team you belong to has been losing recently. You typically wonder, "What's going on?" In each of these cases you assume that there is some factor (or factors) responsible for what is occurring, some *cause* (or causes) that results in the *effect* (or effects) you are observing (the rough engine, the upset stomach, the losing team).

. . . [C]ausality is one of the basic patterns of thinking we use to organize and make sense of our experience. For instance, imagine how bewildered you would feel if a mechanic looked at your car and told you there was no explanation for the poorly running engine. Or suppose you take your upset stomach to the doctor, who examines you and then concludes that there is no possible causal explanation for the malady. In each case you would be understandably skeptical of the diagnosis and would probably seek another opinion.

The Scientific Method

Causal reasoning is also the backbone of the natural and social sciences; it is responsible for the remarkable understanding of our world that has been achieved. The *scientific method* works on the assumption that the world is constructed in a complex web of causal relationships that can be discovered through systematic investigation. Scientists have devised an organized approach for discovering causal relationships and testing the accuracy of conclusions. The sequence of steps is as follows:

1. Identify an event or a relationship between events to be investigated.
2. Gather information about the event (or events).
3. Develop a hypothesis or theory to explain what is happening.
4. Test the hypothesis or theory through experimentation.
5. Evaluate the hypothesis or theory based on experimental results.

How does this sequence work when applied to the situation of the rough-running engine mentioned earlier?

1. *Identify an event or a relationship between events to be investigated.* In this case, the event is obvious—your car's engine is running poorly, and you want to discover the cause of the problem so that you can fix it.

2. *Gather information about the event (or events).* This step involves locating any relevant information about the situation that will help solve the problem. You initiate this step by asking and trying to answer a variety of questions: When did the engine begin running poorly? Was this change abrupt or gradual? When did the car last have a tune-up? Are there other mechanical difficulties that might be related? Has anything unusual occurred with the car recently?

3. *Develop a hypothesis or theory to explain what is happening.* After reviewing the relevant information, you will want to identify the most likely explanation of what has happened. This possible explanation is known as a *hypothesis*. (A theory is normally a more complex model that involves a number of interconnected hypotheses, such as the theory of quantum mechanics in physics.)

Although your hypothesis may be suggested by the information you have, it goes beyond the information as well and so must be tested before you commit yourself to it. In this case the hypothesis you might settle on is "water in the gas." This hypothesis was suggested by

Hypothesis

A possible explanation that is introduced to account for a set of facts and that can be used as a basis for further investigation

your recollection that the engine troubles began right after you bought gas in the pouring rain. This hypothesis may be correct or it may be incorrect—you have to test it to find out.

When you devise a plausible hypothesis to be tested, you should keep three general guidelines in mind:

- *Explanatory power:* The hypothesis should effectively explain the event you are investigating. The hypothesis that damaged windshield wipers are causing the engine problem doesn't seem to provide an adequate explanation of the difficulties.

- *Economy:* The hypothesis should not be unnecessarily complex. The explanation that your engine difficulty is the result of sabotage by an unfriendly neighbor is possible but unlikely. There are simpler and more direct explanations you should test first.

- *Predictive power:* The hypothesis should allow you to make various predictions to test its accuracy. If the "water in the gas" hypothesis is accurate, you can predict that removing the water from the gas tank and gas line should clear up the difficulty.

4. *Test the hypothesis or theory through experimentation.* Once you identify a hypothesis that meets these three guidelines, the next task is to devise an experiment to test its accuracy. In the case of your troubled car, you would test your hypothesis by pouring several containers of "dry gas" into the tank, blowing out the gas line, and cleaning the fuel injection valve. By removing the moisture in the gas system, you should be able to determine whether your hypothesis is correct.

5. *Evaluate the hypothesis or theory based on experimental results.* After reviewing the results of your experiment, you usually can assess the accuracy of your hypothesis. If the engine runs smoothly after you remove moisture from the gas line, then this strong evidence supports your hypothesis. If the engine does *not* run smoothly after your efforts, then this persuasive evidence suggests that your hypothesis is not correct. There is, however, a third possibility. Removing the moisture from the gas system might improve the engine's performance somewhat but not entirely. In that case you might want to construct a *revised* hypothesis along the lines of "Water in the gas system is partially responsible for my rough-running engine, but another cause (or causes) might be involved as well."

If the evidence does not support your hypothesis or supports a revised version of it, you then begin the entire process again by identifying and testing a new hypothesis. The natural and social sciences engage in an ongoing process of developing theories and hypotheses and testing them through experimental design. Many theories and hypotheses are much more complex than our "moisture in the gas" example and take years of generating, revising, and testing. Determining the subatomic structure of the universe and finding cures for various kinds of cancers, for example, have been the subjects of countless theories and hypotheses, as well as experiments to test their accuracy. We might diagram this operation of the scientific process as follows:

Acceptance, rejection, or revision of a theory/hypothesis

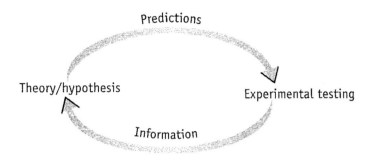

Thinking Activity

APPLYING THE SCIENTIFIC METHOD

Select one of the following situations or describe a situation of your own choosing. Then analyze the situation by working through the various steps of the scientific method listed directly after.

- Situation 1: You wake up in the morning with an upset stomach.
- Situation 2: Your grades have been declining all semester.
- Situation 3: (Your own choosing)

1. *Identify an event or a relationship between events to he investigated.* Describe the situation you have selected.

2. *Gather information about the event (or events).* Elaborate the situation by providing additional details. Be sure to include a variety of possible causes for the event. (For example, an upset stomach might be the result of food poisoning, the flu, anxiety, etc.)

3. *Develop a hypothesis or theory to explain what is happening.* Based on the information you have described, identify a plausible hypothesis or theory that (a) explains what occurred, (b) is clear and direct, and (c) leads to predictions that can be tested.

4. *Test the hypothesis or theory through experimentation.* Design a way of testing your hypothesis that results in evidence proving or disproving it.

5. *Evaluate the hypothesis or theory based on experimental results.* Describe the results of your experiment and explain whether the results lead you to accept, reject, or revise your hypothesis.

3

Chapter 3: Fallacies

Mistakes in Reasoning: The World of Fallacies

Kurt Mosser

What We Will Be Exploring

- We will look at mistakes in reasoning, known as fallacies.
- We will examine how these kinds of mistakes occur.
- We will see that errors in reasoning can take place because of the structure of the argument.
- We will discover that different errors in reasoning arise due to using language illegitimately, requiring close attention be paid to that language.

Generally, we want our arguments to be "good" arguments—sound deductive arguments and strong inductive arguments. Unfortunately, arguments often look good when they are not. Such arguments are said to commit a **fallacy**, a mistake in reasoning. Wide ranges of fallacies have been identified, but we will look at only some of the most common ones. When trying to construct a good argument, it is important to be able to identify what bad arguments look like. Then we can avoid making these mistakes ourselves and prevent others from trying to convince us of something on the basis of bad reasoning!

1 What Is a Fallacy?

Ruth Tomlinson/Photolibrary

The French village of Roussillon at sunrise. Roussillon is in Vaucluse, Provence. It would be a fallacy to assume that because someone lives in France, he or she lives in Paris.

Most simply, a fallacy is an *error in reasoning*. It is different from simply being mistaken, however. For instance, if someone were to say that "2 + 3 = 6," that would be a *mistake*, but it would not be a *fallacy*. Fallacies involve *inferences*, the move from one sentence (or a set of sentences) to another. Here's an example:

> **If I live in Paris, then I live in France.**
>
> **I live in France.**
>
> **Therefore,**
>
> **I live in Paris.**

Here, we have two premises and a conclusion. The first sentence is a conditional, and we can accept it as true. Let's assume the second sentence is also true. But even if those two premises were true, the conclusion would not be true. While it may be true that if I live in Paris then I live in France, and it may be true that I live in France, it *does not follow* that I live in Paris, because I could live in any number of other places in France. Thus, the inference from the premises to the conclusion is *fallacious* because of a mistake in the reasoning. Technically, this argument is said to commit the formal fallacy of "affirming the consequent" of the conditional. In a conditional sentence, "If P then Q," P is the **antecedent**—it provides the condition—and Q is the **consequent**, or what follows from that conditional. So in this sentence, "If I need to get cash, then I can go to an ATM," "I need to get cash" is the antecedent, and "I can go to an ATM" is the consequent.

We can see the difference in the arguments here by looking at a very similar one that does not commit this fallacy (because it affirms the *antecedent*) and is in fact *valid*:

> **If I live in Paris, then I live in France.**
>
> **I live in Paris.**
>
> **Therefore,**
>
> **I live in France.**

In learning to spot fallacies, we must be very careful to see whether the conclusion actually follows from the premises; if it does not, we need to determine why. Sometimes, as in our first argument here, the mistake is structural, or formal. At other times, the mistake is more subtle, and we have to examine the content of the argument—its meaning—to determine why it commits the fallacy; these kinds of mistakes in reasoning are often called "informal fallacies." Here again is the famous informal fallacy we looked at in Chapter 2:

> **Nothing is better than eternal happiness.**
>
> **A ham sandwich is better than nothing.**
>
> **Therefore,**
>
> **A ham sandwich is better than eternal happiness.**

The fallacy involved here is *not* structural; an argument with this structure actually can provide a valid inference, as in this example:

> **Mary is taller than Susan.**
>
> **Susan is taller than Amanda.**
>
> **Therefore,**
>
> **Mary is taller than Amanda.**

Alan Bailey/Photolibrary

The transitive property allows us to infer that if Billy is taller than Sally, and Sally is taller than Jeff, then Billy must be taller than Jeff.

This is an example of what is known as the **transitive property**, as in arithmetic: if 10 is less than 20, and 20 is less than 30, then we know—just from these two sentences—that 10 is less than 30.

In contrast, the mistaken inference in the argument about the ham sandwich involves the *meaning* of the words, specifically the word "nothing." In the first premise, to say there is nothing better than eternal happiness is to say there exists no thing better. But in the second premise, "nothing" seems to change meaning in order to say it is better to have a sandwich than to have nothing (as in the phrase "well, it's better than nothing"). The word "nothing" subtly changes meaning from one sentence to the next, but the argument treats them as if "nothing" means the same thing. This then appears to allow us to draw the conclusion, but the mistake should be clear, and so we see why we cannot, on the basis of these premises, accept the conclusion that a ham sandwich is better than eternal happiness. Thus, the inference is made illegitimately, and that illegitimate inference is what results in a fallacy. While the ham sandwich argument is a bit silly, it is a good example of how, even if we are sure that there is a mistake in the reasoning, it can be a bit tricky to say what, precisely, that mistake is.

There are many formal fallacies, mistakes in reasoning that occur due to the *structure* of the argument (the fallacy of affirming the consequent is, therefore, a formal fallacy). There are also hundreds of informal fallacies. In this chapter, we look at some of the best-known informal fallacies, and a couple of the most common formal fallacies. It is obvious why we want to avoid fallacies as a general rule; after all, fallacies are mistakes, and we want to avoid making mistakes. But here we also consider why we want to avoid the specific kinds of errors committed by fallacious reasoning.

Why Should We Avoid Fallacies?

Matthias Baumgartner/Photolibrary

Fallacies can be like cracks in a building, undermining the strength of our arguments.

We have already seen that philosophers use the term *argument* differently from how we use it in everyday conversation: to a philosopher, an argument simply provides reasons for accepting a conclusion. As we have also seen, our everyday reasoning usually includes a mixture of both deductive and inductive arguments. Obviously enough, when we try to establish a conclusion on the basis of evidence and reasoning, we want our arguments to be *good* arguments: valid (and sound) deductive arguments and strong inductive arguments. Fallacies are, in this context, somewhat like a virus, or a disease. That is, fallacies infect our reasoning and can give an argument the appearance that its conclusion should be accepted when it really shouldn't be. We may never be able to "cure" our reasoning of the fallacies that threaten to infect it, but the more we are aware of the problem, the better our chance of being able to avoid it. Healthy reasoning, then, always requires that we be on the lookout for fallacies; in this case, as the old saying goes, an ounce of prevention is worth a pound of cure.

One clear result of studying and understanding fallacies is that we become aware of the problems they can cause in our own reasoning. Presumably, when we give an argument of our own, we want it to be the best argument we can construct; we assume, that is, that we aren't willing to abandon sound principles of reasoning to win the argument. (There are contexts, of course, where this might not be the case, and we will look at some of these later.) We want to win our arguments, of course, but we also want to construct them correctly. Being aware of the various fallacies will improve our arguments and make them more difficult to defeat. After all, if our opponent in an argument can expose our reasoning as fallacious, our opponent will win, or at least show that our argument fails.

We also, of course, don't want to be fooled by our opponent into accepting reasoning that is not legitimate. Perhaps you are in a debate with someone who argues that raising taxes is bad for the economy. Your opponent points out that the last time taxes were raised, the economy did badly; therefore, raising taxes caused the bad economy. You may want to resist this conclusion, and being aware of fallacies allows you to point out that this argument commits the fallacy of the "false cause": just because some event follows another event, it does not necessarily mean that the first event *caused* the second event. To make this fallacy clear to your opponent, you may provide a counterexample that uses the same kind of logic. "I took my dog for a walk, and then it rained. But walking my dog didn't *cause* it to rain, did it?" Revealing the flawed reasoning in this case doesn't mean that we have established that raising taxes is good for the economy, or that it is bad for the economy. But by demonstrating that the argument commits this fallacy, you can reject this argument as given, and you and your opponent can move on, in order to look for *better* arguments.

3.1 Questions for Review

1. True or false? A fallacy is a legitimate form of reasoning.

2. True or false? Fallacies, unlike simple mistakes, involve inferences.

2 Mistakes in Reasoning: Informal Fallacies

Now that we have seen why we should be aware of fallacies, and why we should try to avoid them, we will identify and examine the most common informal fallacies. These fallacies are frequently encountered at work as well as among friends and family and in the media. For each of these fallacies, we will begin with an example and then specify the mistake involved in each. One of the best ways to become familiar with fallacies, once you understand them, is to construct one of your own that commits the same kind of error.

Ad Hominem Fallacy

> Frank works for a big oil company. So of course, Frank doesn't believe in
> global climate change.

If we put this in premise-conclusion form, the argument would look like this:

Frank works for a big oil company.

Frank doesn't believe in global climate change.

Ken Weingart/Photolibrary

An ad hominem fallacy occurs when the reason for an argument is solely based on a person's character or nature.

The ad hominem fallacy comes from the Latin term for "to the person": that is, the conclusion is to be accepted or rejected because of the person (and the characteristics of that person) involved, rather than the actual argument, or reason(s), supporting the conclusion. In our example, then, the reason put forth for Frank's belief has little to do with the evidence Frank may have for that belief. Rather, the fact that he works for a big oil company provides the basis for why we attribute to Frank the belief we do. Of course, this is fallacious; Frank may have very good reasons, very bad reasons, or no reasons at all for his belief. But the fact that he works for a company that may be adversely affected by the politics of climate change doesn't allow us to conclude that this is the *reason* for Frank's view on the matter. Because this refers to Frank's *circumstances*, this fallacy is often made more precise by labeling it an ad hominem argument (circumstantial). As always with fallacies, the conclusion *does not follow* from the premise(s).

We can see this mistake by a rather ridiculous example. Presuming the communist dictator of the former Soviet Union, Josef Stalin, was a very bad person, what if someone made this argument?

Josef Stalin believes that the sun rises in the east. Stalin was one of the worst monsters of the twentieth century. Therefore, we shouldn't believe that the sun rises in the east.

Clearly, the sun rises in the east regardless of what we think about Stalin; his character certainly doesn't allow us to reject the claim. Here again, we see the reason put forth for the conclusion to be simply about the person involved. But, as should be obvious, even the most tyrannical dictator may hold beliefs that are true. In contrast to the ad hominem (circumstantial), this is a mistake based on the *character* of the person. Stalin's character may well be worth attacking; but his personal failures, in this case, don't have anything to do with whether his belief about the sun is true or not. Hence, we have two distinct kinds of ad hominem arguments: one based on the circumstances of the person, such as Frank's job, and one based on the character of the person, such as Stalin's.

To spot an ad hominem fallacy, we determine whether the reason given for the conclusion rests solely on the characteristics or nature of the person who holds the view in question. And if those characteristics are not relevant to the conclusion, there is a good chance an ad hominem fallacy is being committed. Sometimes, however, those characteristics can be quite relevant, as in the following example:

Mary is a devout Christian, so of course she believes in God.

One of the defining characteristics of being a Christian is to believe in God; so if Mary is a devout Christian, it *does follow* that she believes in God. In this case, unlike the cases of Frank and Stalin, Mary's personal characteristics are quite relevant to the conclusion and provide ample support for it.

One can also consider one other version of this fallacy, often referred to by its Latin name *tu quoque*, meaning, "you're another." We are probably familiar with this fallacy from grade school; if you object to someone's behavior, he or she might respond that your behavior is no better. This reply, of course, does not respond to your objection; rather, the claim seems to be that you can't object because you have your own share of problems. If Robyn objects to Tom cheating on a test, and Tom replies that Robyn cheated on a test once, so she cannot legitimately object, he commits this fallacy.

An actual, historical, example of the tu quoque fallacy was committed by the government of South Africa when it defended its apartheid policy of racial separation and discrimination. In some of its literature sent to the United States, this argument was made by the South African government:

> **The U.S. treated its native citizens very badly, including putting them on reservations.**
>
> **Therefore,**
>
> **The U.S. cannot criticize our treatment of our own native citizens.**

The premise may well be accepted as true here, but it doesn't follow that one cannot still criticize the South African policy. In this case, we may recall the phrase from our childhood, "two wrongs don't make a right."

Hence the ad hominem fallacy is committed when the conclusion is rejected on the basis of characteristics of the person who puts forth the conclusion, *and* the characteristics of that person are not relevant to the conclusion. Once you are aware of the mistake in reasoning involved here, you may be surprised at how often you encounter the ad hominem fallacy.

Stop and Think: Lose It, Don't Abuse It!

Celebrities such as Oprah Winfrey, Dr. Phil, and Suzanne Somers have all written books on nutrition and weight loss. Some critics have dismissed their advice outright, citing Oprah's weight fluctuations ("Why would anyone take diet advice from a dieter who repeatedly fails?"), Dr. Phil's larger physique ("Why would anyone take weight loss advice from Dr. Phil, who seems unable to lose that last 20–30 pounds?"), and the possibility that Somers may not practice what she preaches ("This queen of all things natural fills her face with Botox and the like").

Each of these comments qualifies as ad hominem attacks. For example, whether or not Dr. Phil is a few pounds overweight has no bearing upon the relative merits of his weight loss program.

It may seem quite natural to dismiss a person's claims outright on the basis of ad hominem considerations. An overweight person telling us how to lose weight strikes us as hypocritical, and no one likes a hypocrite. Nonetheless, we must remember that even the biggest hypocrites can, at least on occasion, speak the truth.

As we can see, ad hominem appeals on their own do not demonstrate any weaknesses in these weight loss programs. If so, how *should* one go about assessing the merits of diet advice? What sorts of considerations are, in fact, relevant to such an analysis?

Begging the Question

Abortion is murder, and murder is illegal, so abortion should be illegal.

To beg the question is to commit a mistake in reasoning by assuming what one seeks to prove. Often this kind of reasoning is criticized as "circular reasoning," in that the premise that supports the conclusion is in turn supported by the conclusion, and thus goes in a circle.

Corbis/Photolibrary

To "beg the question" is to make a leap of logic by assuming what needs to be established.

In the preceding argument, we may be quite willing to accept that murder is illegal. But the controversy over abortion really involves the first premise, whether or not abortion qualifies as murder. To assume that abortion is murder, then, begs the question, for that is the very issue that is at stake in the argument.

It is important to see that rejecting this argument because it is fallacious doesn't establish anything about the topic of abortion. Rather, it indicates that this argument, as structured, relies on an illegitimate inference, or commits a fallacy. Thus, it isn't better *as an argument* than the following:

Capital punishment is murder, and murder is illegal, so capital punishment should be illegal.

In this case, one cannot legitimately *assume* that capital punishment is murder; one would have to provide an argument for that premise. Again, this argument doesn't establish anything about capital punishment, because the argument is fallacious. In both the argument about abortion and the argument about capital punishment, we see that because the question is begged, these arguments fail. This doesn't mean that one cannot construct good arguments about either topic, however.

Perhaps we can see this more clearly with a ridiculous argument that has exactly the same structure:

Sunbathing is murder, and murder is illegal, so sunbathing should be illegal.

While many people argue over the ethical and moral questions that surround abortion and capital punishment, probably no one would argue that sunbathing is murder. But all three of these arguments are identical in structure, and now we can see a bit better why that structure is fallacious: we simply cannot legitimately *assume* what we seek to *establish*.

In logic, to beg the question is to assume what one wishes to prove, although one often hears people in the media use the phrase to indicate that one answer leads to another. A politician, for instance, may be told that her response in an interview "begs the question," or that her response raises further issues. This is *not* the precise, technical meaning of the phrase as used in logic, and here, as elsewhere, we will discover that logicians often use language in a way that is much more specific and explicit than it is in other contexts.

It should also be noted that arguments that beg the question, or argue circularly, are technically *valid*. In all three of our examples, *if* the premises are accepted as true, we must accept the conclusion as true. But as we saw most obviously in the sunbathing example, the premise may well *not* be true. This is yet one more reason to remember that just because an argument is valid does not necessarily mean we should accept its conclusion!

Slippery Slope Arguments

We must not allow libraries to ban any books; if they ban some books, they may well ban all of them.

The slippery slope fallacy is committed when one takes an example and extends it indefinitely to show that a given undesirable result will inevitably follow. Often the idea is that if an exception is allowed to a rule, then more and more exceptions will follow, leading to the inevitable result that few people, if any, will follow the rule. But this conclusion isn't always warranted. A library may well wish to prohibit certain kinds of material, such as pornography, but that doesn't mean that libraries will end up banning all kinds of materials.

Here's another example:

The police won't ticket you if you drive one mile an hour over the speed limit.

The police won't ticket you if you drive two miles an hour over the speed limit.

The police won't ticket you if you drive three miles an hour over the speed limit.

Therefore,

The police won't ticket you if you drive n miles an hour over the speed limit.

Eventually, it seems that the police, by making these exceptions, may not be able to ticket anyone no matter how much over the speed limit he or she drives. But that conclusion doesn't follow from these premises; just because there is some degree of tolerance, or minor exceptions to the rule, that does not mean the rule itself is abandoned. And anyone who has gotten a speeding ticket has learned this the hard way!

While these kinds of arguments commit the slippery slope fallacy, there are other ways of making this kind of mistake. Perhaps Rosemary thinks it is fine to have a glass of wine or two at dinner, but Franklin does not. Franklin tells her that if she has a glass of wine at dinner, pretty

Ingram Publishing/Photolibrary

The view from the top of a slide. A slippery slope fallacy takes one example and extends it indefinitely to an unrelated conclusion.

soon she will end up drinking a whole bottle of wine at dinner. There is some point between drinking no wine and drinking too much wine, but the idea that one glass of wine automatically leads to drinking too much wine seems to commit a rather obvious slippery slope fallacy.

Determining whether an argument actually commits the slippery slope fallacy can be difficult. A teacher may make an exception to the rule "no late work is accepted" and allow a student to turn in a paper late. This may have a "snowball effect," because the other students can point to this exception and ask why they aren't also allowed to turn their work in late. Parents who enforce a strict bedtime may also worry that if they make exceptions, the idea of "bedtime" will become so flexible that it will become very difficult to get the kids to bed at a reasonable time.

For these kinds of reasons, some philosophers have argued that certain rules cannot have any exceptions. For instance, consider the rule that you should never lie, that without exception, you should always tell the truth. The concern is that if an exception is made in one case, there may be exceptions in other cases, and eventually no one will be expected to tell the truth. One can see a similar idea with counterfeit money. A society cannot make exceptions, suggesting that sometimes counterfeit money is acceptable, for if even one exception is made, it is clear that we won't possess the needed confidence that the money in circulation is genuine. Thus, to avoid this situation, no exceptions can be made. In this case, we have to be very strict; if some lies are permitted, we may well end up not being able to say where they are *not* permitted. In this case, it could be argued that there is a "cascading" effect where some lying leads to too much lying, and on this view would *not* be a slippery slope fallacy. Similarly, to try to prevent counterfeit money from circulating seems legitimate; there isn't a slippery slope involved in thinking that if some counterfeit money is allowed to circulate, we may have significant problems in determining what is and what is not genuine money.

In general, then, one has to examine the premises of the specific argument to determine if, in fact, they support the conclusion. The premises must be *shown* to lead to the conclusion, and the connection between the premises and conclusion must be demonstrated. If one simply indicates that because one or more exceptions to a rule will lead to a rule being entirely ignored—as we saw in the example of the speeding ticket—then we may well have a slippery slope fallacy on our hands.

3.2 Questions for Review

1. True or false? In Latin, ad hominem means "to the person."

2. Which of the following qualifies as an ad hominem argument?

    A. Mr. Tuning told me to read chapter one, so I better, because he is my teacher.
    B. He probably pours good drinks; he is a bartender, after all.
    C. Mary's comments are always wrong; she sits in the front row and tries to be the teacher's pet.
    D. None of the above.

3. True or false? Facts about a person are *never* relevant to what that person has to say.

4. True or false? The begging-the-question fallacy occurs when one question naturally leads a person to ask another question.

5. True or false? Begging the question is also known as "circular reasoning."

6. What of the following qualifies as begging the question?

    A. My landlord is a liar; therefore, she doesn't tell the truth.
    B. My landlord is wealthy, so I may ask her for a loan.
    C. My landlord owns my home, so she should know where the fuse box is located.
    D. All of the above.

7. True or false? Slippery slope arguments assert that allowing one thing to occur will eventually cause something very undesirable to occur without providing adequate justification for such a causal linkage.

8. Which of the following is an illegitimate slippery slope argument?

    A. If you outlaw guns, then only outlaws will have guns.
    B. Guns don't kill people, people kill people.
    C. If you outlaw prostitution in Nevada, then brothels will be illegal, as well as prostitutes working the street.
    D. None of the above.

Hasty Generalization

**I went to that new restaurant the other day, and I didn't like what I had.
I don't think that restaurant is any good.**

We are probably familiar both with having generalized a bit too quickly ourselves and having heard others do so. The fallacy of hasty generalization is committed when the conclusion is based on insufficient information: a generalization is made too quickly. Thus, here, on the basis of having eaten at a restaurant one time, a very broad conclusion is drawn. Of course, the restaurant may *not* be any good, but one meal on one occasion isn't enough to support that conclusion. The chef could have had a bad night; the restaurant, being new, might still be getting things figured out; it could have just been bad luck. But the conclusion that the restaurant isn't any good *does not follow* from the premise, because the premise doesn't provide sufficient support for that conclusion.

In science, researchers expend considerable effort making sure data samples are large enough, and representative enough, to provide support for the conclusion. For instance, if a medical study seeks to establish a connection between cholesterol and heart disease using a data sample of a few patients, it might just be a coincidence if all the patients have high cholesterol and suffer from heart disease. But if the study involves numerous patients, from a wide variety of backgrounds, ages, and so forth, and all of the patients have both high cholesterol and heart disease, that would offer much stronger support for the view that they are causally related.

iStockphoto/Thinkstock

The hasty generalization fallacy can be summed up in the phrase "to paint with a broad brush," which means to characterize without bothering with details or specifics.

Generally, then, the fallacy of hasty generalization is committed when one has inadequate support for the conclusion, but one still jumps to a conclusion. Consider the following argument, for instance:

I've met a couple of people from China who studied English but were difficult to understand. I don't think Chinese people can learn English well.

Given that there are over a billion people in China, and assuming only one percent of them study English, that would be over ten million Chinese people studying English! To generalize on the basis of two people would be very hasty, indeed. Therefore, the evidence would not adequately support this conclusion, and *would not follow* from the premise as stated.

Often the fallacy of hasty generalization can lead to damaging stereotypes made on the basis of just a few examples. Stereotypes about women, religious groups, minorities, ethnic groups, and so forth are often based on this type of reasoning. Drawing broad and very general conclusions based on insufficient evidence can therefore lead to harmful results, not only for the victim of the stereotype but also for the person doing the stereotyping. For instance, consider this argument:

I had a guy from Peru working for me once, and he always came to work late. I won't be hiring any more people from Peru.

The generalization here, drawn on the basis of a single example, is that all Peruvians come to work late. Not only does this attitude discriminate against an entire group of people, but it also prevents the employer from discovering that Peruvians may be the best workers he ever hired. By making a mistake in reasoning and committing the fallacy of hasty generalization, the employer harms both those being stereotyped and himself.

Argument from False Authority

Albert Einstein was a brilliant man and believed in ghosts. So it seems that ghosts actually exist.

The fallacy committed by appealing to a false authority draws a conclusion based on an authority whose expertise is irrelevant to the conclusion. Just because Einstein was a world-famous physicist doesn't make him a legitimate authority on ghosts. (It isn't really clear whether he did or did not believe in ghosts, by the way.) So the conclusion *does not follow* here, because Einstein doesn't have the right kind of expertise to provide support for it.

Naturally, if we sought Einstein's views on a question in physics, we would be on much safer

Presselect Presselect/Photolibrary

English socialite Tara Palmer-Tomkinson appears in a commercial for potato chips. Celebrities endorse products all the time, and we don't often stop to think that they might not be an authority on such a product.

ground. There is no question that in physics, his authority is legitimate, and we could rely on his expertise. Hence, the name of this fallacy is important: the argument from false authority. In looking at arguments, it is important to determine whether the person whose view is being used to support the conclusion is truly an authority, and if so, whether that authority is *relevant* to the conclusion.

Another way this mistake is often made is to suggest that a source of information has a conflict of interest: a person may benefit from some outcome, and we may think that such a benefit can call that person's claim into question. Imagine a university president arguing that the basketball team should purchase a particular brand of shoes. She claims it is because they are the best shoes one can get at a good price, but she also has substantial holdings in the company that makes the shoes. Are we sure the university president is not biased in promoting the purchase of this brand of shoes? After all, she stands to make more money if the company's stock does well. At the same time, the fact that she owns this stock doesn't mean that the shoes are *not* the best shoe available for the price.

Such conflicts of interest can be very challenging, for it is not that unusual that one's arguments are driven by one's self-interest. But simply because that self-interest may be involved does not mean that the argument definitely is driven by that self-interest. Each case must be looked at carefully. But for this reason, politicians often sell stocks and get rid of other investments in case there may be even an *appearance* of such a conflict of interest. Judges who are asked to decide on cases in which they may have a financial interest frequently recuse themselves: they do not hear such cases just in case it appears that they have such a conflict of interest.

Perhaps the most common version of this argument can be seen in television commercials. For instance:

A world famous golfer says he likes to drive a certain model of car. So that model of car must be pretty great!

Of course, if we stop to think about it, it isn't clear why we should think that being excellent at golf establishes one's credentials in evaluating automobiles. Similarly, basketball players may not know any better than we do if a given fast-food restaurant is particularly good, and there is no reason to think that a famous football player is an expert on jeans. Yet it is hard to turn on a television without seeing a celebrity endorse a product, lending their reputation for expertise in their own field to a product they are paid to advertise. In such cases, the conclusion—that a product is good—*does not follow* from the premise; namely, that a celebrity whose fame comes from a completely different area of life *says* it is good.

On occasion, a celebrity may actually be an authority in another field. For example, a movie star who is an expert chef may recommend a certain brand of kitchen knife. If she says the knife is good, we could accept her recommendation if (and only if) we were also able to determine that she was an authority in the relevant field. But the fallacy of appealing to an illegitimate authority is committed when the support provided by the authority is not relevant.

When examining an argument that appeals to an authority, we must see what the credentials are of the authority and whether those credentials are relevant to the conclusion being put forth. This may not always be clear-cut; if a physician runs for political office, does her expertise in medicine indicate expertise in making quality political decisions? Do the kinds of questions physicians deal with give them advantages in making political decisions? Or are political and medical decisions so distinct that expertise in medicine is irrelevant to expertise in politics? In such cases, we need to learn more about the candidate in question and whether the candidate possesses the appropriate background, credentials, and expertise. But we may see why identifying someone as a good doctor may well not be sufficient to make that person a good political leader.

Appeals to Pity and Popularity

Your honor, I'm innocent. I haven't been able to find work for several months, and I've been very sick. So I shouldn't be found guilty.

That book must be very good; it has been on the best-seller list for weeks.

Two related fallacies, the appeal to pity and the appeal to popularity, make very similar mistakes in reasoning. In the appeal to pity, the reason put forth doesn't give a good reason to accept the conclusion, but considers what, logically, is irrelevant information. The appeal to pity indicates that one should accept a conclusion because of the unfortunate situation of the person putting forth that conclusion. In the same way, in the appeal to popularity, the reason put forth doesn't give a good reason to accept the conclusion, but considers what is irrelevant information. The appeal to popularity indicates that a conclusion should be accepted simply because many people think it is true. In both cases, of course, the conclusion *does not follow* from the premises. Someone accused of a crime isn't innocent of the crime just because he or she is in bad circumstances; rather, guilt or innocence is based on whether the person actually committed the crime. Similarly, a book isn't good just because it is popular; presumably we want to evaluate a book's quality by characteristics *other* than just its popularity. As we know, sometimes books that are not very good sell many copies, just as some very good books do not sell many copies.

Teachers frequently encounter the appeal to pity, but they also encounter arguments that seem to commit this fallacy but actually do not. Compare the following two arguments:

I need to get an A in this course, because if I don't, I will lose my scholarship.

I couldn't get my paper turned in on time, because there was a tornado and all the power went out.

The first argument appeals to pity by suggesting that the reason the student should get an A is that if he doesn't, he will lose his scholarship. That

Creatas/Photolibrary

Appeals to pity (and popularity) can lead to true or false conclusions. The key is determining whether the conclusion follows from the premises.

conclusion, of course, does not follow; he should get an A if his work deserves it. Presumably, it is not just this course that is leading to this result, anyway. The second argument appears to offer a similar kind of reasoning, but, in fact, such a power outage might well be a *legitimate* reason for a late paper.

Similarly, an appeal to popularity may not always lead to a false conclusion; again, we have to determine whether the conclusion follows from what is being stated.

> **The pizza in that place must be great; it always has a long line of customers.**

Of course, the reason the pizza is good isn't *because* the pizza place has a long line of customers; the reason the pizza is good is because, well, it's good! But one might see that there is another premise here, one that is not explicitly stated: customers line up only for a product that is really good. In that case, if there is a long line of customers, and customers are willing to stand in line only for something that is good, then a long line of customers for this pizza suggests that it is good.

In both of these fallacies, then, one must look at the premises and see if they support the conclusion; as always, the question is, does the conclusion follow from those premises? There may be "hidden" premises, as we saw in the pizza case, or there may not be. But after looking at the information provided, if the reason to accept a given conclusion is *solely* because of the sad circumstances of the person putting forth the conclusion, that argument may well commit the fallacy of the appeal to pity. And, in the same way, if the reason to accept a given conclusion is *solely* because a lot of people accept it, the argument may well commit the fallacy of the appeal to popularity.

Logic in the Real World:

The "Dying Card"

As we have learned, not all arguments that may touch us on an emotional level are necessarily fallacious. Television satirist Stephen Colbert provides a good example in an interview with a doctor promoting the value of having children immunized. According to the doctor, "[if we don't immunize children] every year we would have thousands of children dying from measles or whooping cough, or we'd have congenital birth defects from rubella or [children] being paralyzed by polio."

To this, Colbert replied, "See, now this isn't fair because you're playing the children dying card. How am I supposed to fight that? Let's keep this intellectual."

What Colbert is doing here is *falsely* accusing the doctor of using an appeal to pity in his statement. The doctor's reference to potential child mortality *is* relevant to the question of immunization, and his mention of this possibility does not take his argument out of the realm of intellectual analysis, as claimed by Colbert.

Arguments that may move heartstrings may or may not be fallacious; it is up to us to figure out whether or not we are encountering legitimate reasoning. This can sometimes prove difficult. Can you think of any ways to help us determine if an argument that invokes an emotional response is in fact fallacious? Are such arguments more difficult to assess accurately? Why or why not?

1. Which of the following most accurately characterizes the fallacy of hasty generalization?

   A. A case where a generalization is accepted based upon sufficient information
   B. A case where a generalization is rejected based upon sufficient information
   C. A case where a generalization is made based upon insufficient information
   D. None of the above

2. True or false? One of the dangers of hasty generalizations is that they can lead to false stereotypes.

3. True or false? All generalizations are fallacious.

4. Which of the following qualifies as an argument from false authority?

   A. My plumber said that my pipes should last for many years, so I'm going to use the money I set aside to fix them to instead go on a vacation.
   B. My vet said that my headaches may be caused by the radiation given off by my cell phone, so I'm going to stop using it.
   C. My dentist told me that I have a cavity that needs filling, so I guess I will have to face the fact that I should go under the drill soon.
   D. All of the above.

5. True or false? Sometimes, a person who may not appear to be an authority on a certain topic may still make correct assertions that concern that topic.

6. True or false? The fact that many people believe something is the case is always sufficient reason to believe it is the case.

7. True or false? The appeal to pity fallacy applies to cases where we are urged to accept a claim made by a person only on the basis of some dire circumstance the person is in or will suffer.

8. True or false? The existence of "hidden" premises is irrelevant in determining whether an appeal to pity or popularity is being used.

Loaded Question

> I asked Susan the other day if she had stopped smoking marijuana. She
> said no, so she must still be smoking marijuana.

The fallacy of the loaded question is committed when separate questions are combined unfairly. The resulting question cannot be answered without accepting an unfair assumption. If I were to ask Susan this question and she said "yes," then that would lead to the conclusion that she did smoke marijuana but has now stopped. If I were to ask Susan this question and she said "no," then that would lead to the conclusion that she did smoke marijuana and continues to do so. But these aren't really fair alternatives for Susan because of the way the question is worded.

In this example, what is "disguised" is that there are really *two* questions:

1. **Have you smoked marijuana?**
2. **If so, have you stopped?**

Clearly enough, if the answer to the first question here is "no," then the second question doesn't apply. By combining the two questions into one question, it illegitimately assumes that the person has been doing the activity in question. In this way, the fallacy of the loaded question can be associated with a fallacy we saw earlier, that of begging the question, because both involve a false premise: in the current example, it is illegitimate to assume that the person ever smoked marijuana. In response to this question, Susan should have pointed out that it is unfairly worded, and that it assumes something that cannot be legitimately assumed.

A question itself, of course, is not an argument, but if the question leads to a conclusion, it can provide the materials for an argument, as we can see in this example:

> **Chris: I don't support affirmative action.**
>
> **Bob: Chris, why don't you support equal opportunities for women and minorities?**

Bob's implied argument, when broken down, looks like this:

> **Chris is against affirmative action.**
>
> **Therefore,**
>
> **Chris is against equal opportunities for women and minorities.**

When looked at this way, it is clear that Bob is assuming that affirmative action is necessary for women and minorities to receive equal opportunities. Affirmative action may be necessary for those opportunities, and it may not be; the point is that Bob cannot simply *assume* that it is necessary. Rather, he has to *argue* for the point, and by wording the question in the way he does, he makes an illegitimate assumption. For this reason, such questions are also frequently called "complex questions" because the question is, in fact, more complex than it may appear. As always, we see that when a fallacy is committed, the conclusion of the argument (whether that argument is explicit or merely implied) *does not follow* from the premises, or the reasons given, for that conclusion.

Straw Man Fallacy

Senator Jones wants to cut defense spending. I guess he doesn't care if we can't protect ourselves.

The straw man fallacy takes an opponent's claim, characterizes that claim unfairly, and then criticizes the opponent on the basis of that unfair characterization. In addition to not really addressing the opponent's claim, the straw man fallacy also draws a conclusion by criticizing a different position than that advocated by the opponent. For that reason, the conclusion *does not follow* from the premise. In our example, there may be a significant difference between cutting defense spending by some percentage and having an inadequate defense. Presumably, one can argue that a country can, or cannot, still defend itself while spending less. Of course, whether or not that is the case is not the issue here; what is at issue is what Senator Jones's claim actually is. Here, the claim seems to be mischaracterized, then criticized on that basis. This sets up a "straw

Heiner Heine/Photolibrary

A jousting reenactment in Germany. Characterizing an opponent's claim unfairly essentially sets up a "dummy" argument that is easy to knock down and doesn't fight back.

man"—an unfair description of an opponent's viewpoint—and then that straw man is "knocked down"—by criticizing not the view actually put forth, but the view as unfairly represented.

Amy thinks the way factory farms raise chickens is cruel. Amy must think we can live on just nuts and berries.

Amy's position here is that certain methods of raising chickens involve some degree of cruelty. But her position here is mischaracterized to imply that she thinks all methods of food production involving animals involve cruelty; this seems to imply, further, that since cruelty is wrong, all such methods should be prohibited. Thus, her opponent concludes that Amy believes everyone should eat solely "nuts and berries," or, at least, follow a vegetarian or vegan diet. But clearly enough, Amy's claim isn't fairly characterized, and thus what might be implied by that characterization is an illegitimate inference. Attributing a view to Amy, then criticizing her on the basis of that attribution, is a mistake in reasoning. The premise in this kind of argument is not fair to Amy, because it misrepresents her position (thus setting up a straw man). The conclusion based on that premise, then, *does not follow* from Amy's own claim; it follows only from this unfair description of her claim (thus, knocking down the straw man).

If we were to put this argument into premise-conclusion form, the fallacy committed becomes even clearer, and the bracketed premises—not stated in the original argument— show the mistaken assumption being made:

Amy thinks it is cruel to raise chickens on factory farms.

[Raising animals on factory farms is cruel.]

[Most of the animals we eat are raised on factory farms.]

[We should not do what is cruel.]

[The only way to avoid this kind of cruelty is not to eat animals.]

Therefore,

Amy thinks we should live on just nuts and berries (that is, not eat animals).

It is probably clear that this could very well mischaracterize Amy's position; there are, for instance, ways of raising animals for food that are not cruel. But by providing the specifics of the argument here, we can see that a number of assumptions are being made— although not stated in the original argument—that one (Amy, for one) might well challenge or dispute.

The trick with the straw man fallacy, however, is that there can be serious disputes about what is and isn't a fair characterization of an opponent's view. In our preceding examples there may be legitimate disputes about whether Senator Jones is proposing cuts to defense spending that risk weakening the military too much. There may also be disagreements with Amy, about whether there is in fact cruelty involved in factory farming, and if there is, how much cruelty is involved. The straw man fallacy is committed when it is obvious that an opponent's position is being criticized based on a clearly unfair characterization of that position. But there may be legitimate disagreement about whether the opponent's position is being unfairly represented.

Two Frameworks You Can Use to Help Identify Fallacies

Fallacies can be difficult to identify. Putting arguments into premise-conclusion form, or equation form as it is sometimes called, can help you identify the connection between the premises and the conclusion; in other words, the relevance, or the logic. Some fallacies, like ad hominem, red herring, and straw man, occur more frequently in debates between two people; identifying them can be a little trickier. Following are two frameworks you can use to identify and distinguish between some of the fallacies you've learned about here. We'll use some of the examples that are scattered throughout the chapter to illustrate two frameworks in action.

First, try to figure out if the fallacy occurs in someone's response to another person's argument or claim. If it does, use the "Debate" framework below. Otherwise, use the "Premise-Conclusion" framework.

Debate Framework

1. Identify the issue. Try to plug it into the following sentence: "The arguable issue is whether or not . . ."

2. **Identify person A's argument: both the conclusion and the premises.**
3. **Identify person B's response to person A's argument or claim.**

Does B attack A's character in an attempt to discount the argument? That's an ad hominem fallacy.

Does B distort A's claim in an attempt to make it ridiculous, easier to "knock down"? That's a straw man fallacy.

Does B bring in another issue attempting to distract from A's argument or claim? That's a red herring fallacy.

Premise-Conclusion Framework

1. **Identify the conclusion. Figure out what one is being persuaded to believe or do. Look for conclusion indicator words.**
2. **Identify the reasons offered in support. Look for premise indicator words.**
3. **Put the statements in premise-conclusion form, so the logic is easier to evaluate.**
4. **Compare what you get to the generic forms listed on this site: http://www.nizkor .org/features/fallacies**

Examples:

I went to that new restaurant the other day, and I didn't like what I had. I don't think that restaurant is any good.

> **P: I went to the new restaurant and did not like what I had. (insufficient evidence)**
> **C: Therefore, their food is not good. (overgeneralization)**

Albert Einstein was a brilliant man and believed in ghosts. So it seems that ghosts actually exist.

> **P: Albert Einsten was a brilliant man.**
> **P: Albert Einstein believed in ghosts.**
> **P: Therefore, ghosts exist.**

That book must be very good; it has been on the best-seller list for weeks.

> **P: That book is popular.** -
> **C: Therefore, it must be very good.**

False Cause (Post Hoc) Fallacy

> **The day before the election, the candidate decided to wear her clothes inside out. Since she won, that must have caused her victory.**

If one thing causes another thing to happen, the first event, of course, precedes the second event. For instance, if I put a pot of water on very high heat and the water then boils, we generally are willing to say the heating of the water caused it to boil.

However, *just* because one thing precedes another does not mean the first *causes* the second. To use the terms we saw earlier, for one thing to cause another, it is a *necessary* condition

4X5 Coll-Ong & Associates/Photolibrary

Lucky talismans, like a rabbit foot, often result in false cause fallacies.

that the cause precede the effect. But one thing preceding another is not a *sufficient* condition to establish a causal relationship between the two things, as this example should make clear:

> **Every morning the rooster crows, and then the sun comes up. The rooster, therefore, must cause the sun to come up.**

To claim that one thing causes another solely because it occurs first is to commit the false cause fallacy. Another, more traditional name for this fallacy also reveals the mistake made in the reasoning: "post hoc, ergo propter hoc"—that is, "after this, therefore because of this."

Superstitions are a standard example of the false cause fallacy. If my luck improves (or at least doesn't get any worse) when I carry around a rabbit's foot, or when I tie my right shoe before tying my left shoe, or when I avoid walking under ladders, then I may be tempted to say that these practices caused or helped cause my good luck. But there are a couple of problems here. First, my luck could always be *worse*, so it is very difficult to tell that such superstitions really caused the results involved. Imagine I carry around a lucky penny, but I am badly injured when run over by a car. Yet my luck could have still been worse: perhaps I reason that if I had not had my lucky penny, I would have been killed by the car. But, more important, we might have difficulty establishing a causal relationship between a superstitious act and the luck that follows, were we to put it to a scientific test. And such a test, of course, would include making quite specific what such "luck" actually involved.

In looking at cause and effect, we might want to distinguish among coincidences, correlations, and causes. If it rains after I wash my car, it may just be an unhappy accident (this would be a coincidence). If this happens with surprising frequency, I may think that it seems to rain almost every time I wash my car (this would be a **correlation**). But do we ever get to the point where we wish to claim that washing my car *causes* it to rain?

Those who study the methods employed by science often try to determine whether a correlation actually supports the strong idea of a causal connection, as we see with this example:

> **Every day after a full moon, the stock market goes up 10 percent. So the full moon causes the stock market to go up 10 percent.**

Here we may be tempted to think of this relationship as a mere coincidence, and that to make the stronger causal claim would be to commit the false cause fallacy. After all, just because the stock market went up after a full moon does not, by itself, indicate that the full moon *caused* it to go up. But what if someone noticed that there was a historical connection and went back through the records to discover that this relationship was very frequent— that almost every time the moon was full, the stock market then went up 10 percent the next day? How do we determine whether this correlation was not just coincidence, but a genuine causal relationship? At this point, of course, we move from logic to actual scientific inquiry, carefully examining the data and testing it in various ways.

In general, we have to carefully state what the evidence is and what conclusion is being drawn, and we must examine the relationship, if any, that exists between the evidence and the conclusion. The fallacy of false cause is committed if we take a sequence of events—one thing followed by another—as by itself establishing a causal relationship. Just because B follows A, it does not follow that A causes B. And if we assert this conclusion on no other basis than the sequence "A then B," we make a mistaken inference and, thus, commit the fallacy of the false cause.

Red Herring

Officer, you shouldn't give me a speeding ticket. There are a lot of people out there who are much more dangerous than I am, and you should be chasing them, not me.

The red herring fallacy is a very old mistake in reasoning—discussions of it go back at least to Aristotle—and also a very common one. A red herring fallacy is committed by someone who tries to avoid the issue by introducing another, irrelevant issue, hoping that it will then attract attention away from the issue that *should* be discussed. As we can see in this example, whether or not the driver deserves a speeding ticket should be determined by whether he or she was speeding. But by introducing the idea of those who break the law in more threatening ways, the driver hopes to divert the attention away from the question of whether he or she was speeding. The fallacy involved here can be made explicit by putting the example in premise-conclusion form:

There are worse crimes than speeding.

Therefore,

I shouldn't be given a ticket for speeding.

As always with the fallacies we have been looking at, we see that the conclusion *does not follow* from the premise. While it certainly is true that there are many worse crimes than speeding, that doesn't mean the driver was *not* speeding. Whether or not a speeding ticket should be given, therefore, has to be argued on a different basis.

Parents are quite familiar with this kind of fallacy. Imagine Suzy says,

You shouldn't make me be home by midnight, Mom. None of my friends has to be home by midnight.

Thinkstock

Smoked fish. Like a smelly fish, a red herring is an irrelevant issue designed to throw the opponent off the true scent of the argument.

To see the fallacy involved, we can put this into premise-conclusion form as well:

None of my friends has to be home by midnight.

Therefore,

I should not have to be home by midnight.

Parents, of course, have a traditional response to this argument (it might be worth considering if a fallacy is committed in this response!):

If all of your friends jumped off a bridge, would you?

Whether or not Suzy's friends have to be home by midnight is irrelevant; the question is whether *Suzy* has to be home by midnight. By getting the parents to address the issue of other children and other rules set down by their parents, Suzy may hope to distract her own parents from their point and get them to focus on other issues.

The red herring fallacy is one example of numerous fallacies that fall under the more general title of "fallacies of irrelevance" (the argument from false authority is another fallacy of irrelevance). All fallacies make the same general mistake in reasoning, leading to the overall result that the conclusion *does not follow* from the premise, or premises. Many fallacies make similar *kinds* of errors; for instance, all fallacies of irrelevance use premises that are irrelevant to the conclusion. It can get confusing keeping the various names and sub-fallacies straight, but it is more important to see *that* a fallacy is committed, and to be able to explain *what* mistake is involved.

Logic in the Real World:

Red Shark Fin

Shark fin soup, thought to have curative powers, has a long tradition in Chinese culture. However, some fear overharvesting is causing a dangerous decline in shark populations, not to mention the cruel and wasteful practice of throwing sharks back into the water after removal of the fins. A legislator in San Francisco—home to the largest Chinatown in the United States—recently proposed a city-wide ban on shark fin sales and possession. Another legislator stated in an opposing response,

> **It seems that there are more and more examples where individuals or groups of individuals are trying to limit our heritage and our culture. It was not so many years ago that, if you happened to be Chinese, you could not go to school outside of Chinatown.**

Preventing Chinese students from going to school outside of Chinatown would be wrong. However, we can see that this matter has nothing at all to do with the issue at hand—that is, whether measures should be taken to stop the slaughter of sharks for their fins. In this response, the opposition threw up a smokescreen in attempting to divert our attention toward Chinese children of San Francisco and away from sharks.

When analyzing arguments, it is important for us always to keep our focus upon the *real* issue. Doing so is the only way we can ensure that nothing "fishy" slips past us!

In the specific case of the red herring, what reveals the error in the argument is the idea that a tangent, or irrelevant issue, is introduced, designed to distract one's opponent from the issue at hand. Before we assert that the red herring fallacy has been committed, therefore, we must show that an irrelevant issue is being introduced as a distraction. In the following example, we see that one person's "red herring" might be another person's genuine concern about a relevant issue. For instance, imagine in a political campaign that one candidate, Ms. Smith, says this about her opponent Mr. Brown:

My worthy opponent Mr. Brown advocates policies that will require more government interference in our lives, and thus should be rejected.

There may be several fallacies involved here (possibly a slippery slope fallacy, for instance). But Mr. Brown might respond that the focus should be on the specific policies in question; from his perspective, Ms. Smith's introduction of the topic of government interference may be intended as a red herring that distracts her audience from those policies. Ms. Smith, on the other hand, might think "government interference" is an important implication of the policies Mr. Brown advocates. So here we can see that although logic can help us identify when a fallacy is committed, logic cannot provide a complete account. In this case, what needs to be argued is whether Ms. Smith's introduction of the topic of government interference is relevant (and thus not a red herring) or not relevant (and thus, as distracting from the issue at hand, is a red herring). Logic by itself is not in a position to settle that dispute!

Logic in the Real World:

The Top Three "Debate" Fallacies in Action

Some fallacies, like ad hominem, red herring, and straw man, are ones that occur in debates between two people. Here we will illustrate the difference between these three, using a single issue: Should marijuana be legalized?

Ad Hominem: Person B Discounts Person A's Argument by Focusing on Character

Person A: I think marijuana should be legalized, because it would rid the prison population of many nonviolent offenders, and that would save us money.

Person B: Of course you'd say that, you're a pot head!

Straw Man: Person B Distorts Person A's Argument to Make It Easier to Knock Down

Person A: I think marijuana should be legalized, because it would rid the prison population of many nonviolent offenders, and that would save us money.

Person B: You think we should legalize drugs?! That's ridiculous!

Red Herring: Person B Distracts from Person A's Argument by Bringing in Another Issue

Person A: I think marijuana should be legalized, because it would rid the prison population of many nonviolent offenders, and that would save us money.

Person B: So you think nonviolent criminals shouldn't be in prison!

> **Emma doesn't think prayer should be allowed in public schools. Therefore, Emma must be an atheist.**

The fallacy of the false dichotomy is also known as the fallacy of "the false dilemma" and the fallacy of "black and white thinking." The mistake in reasoning committed here is to present two, and only two, choices, when in fact there may be many other options available. For instance, in the preceding example, there may be many people who are not atheists who do not support prayer in public schools. To suggest that there are only two options—support for such prayers or atheism—is to ignore the many other options available. Therefore, the conclusion *does not follow* from the premise and commits the fallacy of the false dichotomy.

We saw an earlier argument that committed the fallacy of the straw man—when Amy's view was misrepresented and then criticized on the basis of that misrepresentation:

> **Amy thinks the way factory farms raise chickens is cruel. Amy must think we can live on just nuts and berries.**

Martin Heitner/Photolibrary

A false dichotomy fallacy suggests that there are *only* two options.

This argument also commits the fallacy of the false dichotomy, in that it is at least implied that either one completely ignores how animals are raised for food, or one must advocate vegetarianism. But, of course, one can be a carnivore and care about the treatment of animals. So this argument commits *both* the straw man fallacy *and* the fallacy of the false dichotomy. Either mistake is sufficient to reject the argument as stated, but it is good to keep in mind that a bad argument may make more than one mistake!

On occasion, one may be presented with a choice in which there really is no third option. For instance, in the following example, we seem *not* to commit the fallacy of the false dichotomy, for there truly are only two possibilities (if we exclude vampires):

> **Nick is either dead or alive.**
>
> **Nick is not dead.**
>
> **Therefore,**
>
> **Nick is alive.**

To understand the fallacy of the false dichotomy, then, we must examine the premises. If the premises present a false choice, by ignoring other options, then the conclusion will not follow from the premises as stated. This can sometimes take some care, and we need to be aware that some seemingly persuasive arguments upon closer examination are fallacious. For instance, one may encounter the following bumper sticker:

> **America—Love It or Leave It**

The implied argument here seems to be that certain actions that might be critical of America would indicate that one doesn't love America. The argument would then look something like this in premise-conclusion form:

You must either love America or you must leave America.

If you criticize America, you don't love America.

You have criticized America.

Therefore,

You must leave America.

However, the argument implied by this bumper sticker seems to present two options when there are many others. One might, for instance, want to improve America and thus offer criticism as a way of improving it. Similarly, one might criticize one's spouse and children while also loving them. There may be debates over what is and is not justifiable criticism; but in this case, it seems that one is presented with two choices, when actually there are other choices available. If that is the case, then, this argument would falsely present two choices and would then derive its conclusion on the basis of those two, and only those two, choices. Because there are more choices, this is a mistake in reasoning, an inference is made illegitimately, and the conclusion *does not follow* from the premises.

3.4 Questions for Review

1. True or false? The "loaded question" fallacy refers to questions that are so theoretical in nature they are impossible to understand.

2. Choose the correct name for the following fallacy example:

   Child to Mother: Please, please, I know it is unsupervised, but let me go to the sleepover. I will be devastated if I can't be there!

   A. Ad hominem
   B. Begging the question
   C. Appeal to pity
   D. Loaded question

3. The straw man fallacy

   A. is a false representation of an opponent's position.
   B. is a correct representation of an opponent's position.
   C. is a false claim about an opponent's place of birth.
   D. None of the above

4. True or false? To accurately determine whether a straw man argument is being used, it is important to have a solid understanding of the *actual* view of the opponent in question.

5. Label the following argument:

   I know my boyfriend really loves me. I know this because he told me so, and he would not tell me unless he really loved me.

A. Appeal to popularity
B. Begging the question
C. Appeal to pity
D. Straw man fallacy

6. The false cause fallacy involves

A. falsely accusing someone of a crime.
B. falsely causing something immoral to happen.
C. falsely claiming that a certain person is innocent of a crime.
D. None of the above

7. True or false? Superstitions qualify as examples of the false cause fallacy.

8. Select the correct label for the following fallacy example:

If environmentalists have their way, automobiles will be banished from the earth!

A. False cause
B. Ad hominem
C. Loaded question
D. Straw man

9. True or false? The red herring fallacy is primarily a fallacy of *irrelevance*.

10. Select the correct label for the following fallacy example:

There is no need for the UN to take a stronger role in the enforcement of international human rights. The human rights record of the United States has been good for decades.

A. Red herring
B. Straw man
C. Appeal to popularity
D. Loaded question

11. True or false? The false dichotomy occurs when someone asserts that there are only two options when in fact there may be more.

12. True or false? A case when there really *are* only two alternatives is not an example of the false dichotomy fallacy.

What Did We Find?

- We discovered many arguments that may appear to be persuasive actually commit fallacies.
- We saw that fallacies can occur for various reasons.
- We examined how one identifies the kinds of mistakes made by fallacious arguments.
- We found that being aware of fallacious arguments can help us avoid them in our own reasoning, and also help us spot when others are using such arguments against us.

Some Final Questions

- Consider some of the commercials you've seen. How might such commercials have employed fallacious reasoning to convince you to buy something?
- Try to come up with the kind of argument you might see a politician make. What fallacies do you see committed by some politicians? Why do you think such fallacies seem to be so common in politics?
- Are most people aware of fallacies? How can it improve one's own arguments to be aware of fallacious reasoning? How can understanding fallacies help prevent us from being taken in by arguments that look good at first but are not?

Web Links

The Nizkor project

Visit this site for additional examples of logical fallacies.

http://www.nizkor.org/features/fallacies/

Answers to Questions for Review

3.1

1. False. Just the opposite: fallacies are always *illegitimate* forms of reasoning.
2. True. Fallacies employ faulty inferences in a failed attempt to demonstrate how one sentence leads to another.

3.2

1. True. This hints at the fact that the ad hominem fallacy involves attacks on the person, rather than the person's actual reasoning.
2. **C.** Where Mary chooses to sit in the classroom has no bearing upon the veracity of her comments. This is an ad hominem attack on Mary rather than a legitimate critique of what she says in class.
3. False. Personal characteristics can be relevant in certain cases, and references to them in such instances are not ad hominem attacks.

4. False. While this is a popular usage of this term, it is not the same nor related to the begging the question fallacy.
5. True. In cases of begging the question, the conclusion of an argument is offered as a premise in support of itself, leading to an endless "circle" of reasoning.
6. **A.** If I am arguing that my landlord is a liar, I cannot legitimately use "she is a liar" as a premise in my argument. Doing so results in a circle where nothing is proven at all.
7. True. The strong possibility that one "exception to a rule" will lead to many more must be demonstrated, else we have a case of the slippery slope fallacy.
8. **D.** Both A and B are slogans, and do not assert any illegitimate causal connections regarding one exception causing another. C is simply a true causal claim.

3.3

1. **C.** Hasty generalizations are generalizations based upon an insufficiently small sample size.
2. True. Beliefs about an entire group of people that are based upon exposure to just a few members of the group can cause unfair stereotyping.
3. False. Generalizations based upon sufficiently large and diverse sample groups can be trustworthy and informative. Science, when it is done well, often provides us with examples of legitimate, *non*-hasty generalizations.
4. **B.** While your vet may be an expert on your *pet's* well-being, he or she is likely not an authority on such contentious human medical issues as the ill effects (if any) of cell phone usage.
5. True. A person could certainly offer a lucky and correct guess. Moreover, since people sometimes have hidden expertise in a given area, we would be wrong to dismiss anyone's claims outright just because they are *not* a known authority.
6. False. If you believe something based only upon its popularity, you have fallen prey to the "appeal to popularity" fallacy.
7. True. While emotional response to a person's plight is normal and can demonstrate compassion, it alone does not support the veracity of what they are asserting.
8. False. On the contrary, paying attention to any unstated but implied premises can be a valuable indicator of whether or not the premises support the conclusion.

3.4

1. False. Loaded questions are questions that cannot be answered without committing oneself to a negative position or practice.
2. **C.** Here the child is trying to make a case for her mother to grant permission. However, the only premise offered (a report of her emotional state if she is denied permission) is irrelevant to the conclusion she is urging.
3. **A.** The person guilty of this fallacy creates an easily argued-against misrepresentation of an opponent's viewpoint and argues against *this*, rather than debating the opponent's actual position.
4. True. This knowledge is crucial, because if the characterization of the opponent's position is in fact accurate, a straw man is *not* being made.
5. **B.** This qualifies as begging the question, because the assertion "he really loves me" is being used as a premise to support the conclusion "he really loves me." The result is a clear case of circular reasoning.
6. **D.** The false cause fallacy is the mistaken assumption that simply because one event preceded another in time, the first event must be the cause of the second.
7. True. Superstitions commonly attribute some effect (good luck) to some prior cause (carrying a rabbit's foot) when the "cause" has no actual causal powers.
8. **D.** The vast majority of people who call themselves "environmentalists" do not push for the complete banishment of cars. Thus, this is a false characterization of environmentalism; a straw man set up to be easily "knocked down"/refuted.
9. True. The red herring is a device used in an attempt to avoid the real issue. The method is to shift the focus away from the actual issue by diverting it toward an irrelevant and unrelated consideration.
10. **A.** Even if the human rights record in the United States has been good, it has no relevance to the question of whether the UN should step up efforts to enforce human rights violations on an *international* scale. Thus, the premise is irrelevant to the conclusion, which is a case of the red herring fallacy.
11. True. This is also known as "either/or" as well as "black or white" thinking.
12. True. In such a case, the "either/or" premise is true and is relevant to the conclusion of the argument.

4

Chapter 4: Critical Thinking in Morality

from The Power of Critical Thinking

Lewis Vaughn

We have come far. We have seen that we can productively apply critical thinking to every-day claims, arguments, and problems; to explanations in a wide range of subject areas; to scientific theories of all sorts; and to offbeat theories of the paranormal and supernatural kind. Now we can go even further. We can now venture into a vast and complex sphere that is often thought to be off limits to critical reasoning: *morality*. Morality concerns beliefs about right and wrong, good and bad, and just and unjust. It's an aspect of life that we deal with every day because we have little choice. In countless situations we must decide what we ought to do or not do, what is moral or immoral, and what is good or bad. To do these things, we are forced to accept or reject moral statements, make and criticize moral arguments, and wrestle with moral theories.

In this process of contending with moral issues, we inevitably formulate our own moral the-ory—our own beliefs about what morality is or is not, what actions are right or wrong, and what things are good or bad. To an astonishing degree, our moral theory charts the course of our lives. If the course matters, then we must try to fashion the best moral theory we can.

If we are to be intellectually mature, we also must try to integrate the results of these moral analyses and deliberations into a comprehensive picture of reality, what is known as a worldview. A **worldview** is a philosophy of life, a set of beliefs and theories that helps us make sense of a wide range of issues in life. It defines for us what exists, what should be, and what we can know. We all have a worldview, and our notions about morality are an important part of it. A good critical thinker tries to ensure that his or her worldview contains no internal contradictions and that it offers reliable guidance in dealing with the world.

So in this chapter, we set out to apply critical thinking to some big ideas and broad ques-tions. We explore procedures for evaluating moral discourse—specifically, moral judgments, principles, arguments, and theories—and look at ways that we can incorporate our under-standing into a coherent worldview.

Moral Arguments

A moral argument, like any other kind of argument, has premises and a conclusion. The premises (and sometimes the conclusion) may be implied, not stated, and they may be simple or complex—just as in other arguments. Moral arguments, however, differ from non-moral ones in that their conclusions are moral statements. In general, a moral statement is a statement asserting that an action is right or wrong (moral or immoral) or that something (such as a person or motive) is good or bad. Here are some moral statements:

- Serena should keep her promise to you.
- It is wrong to treat James so harshly.
- Abortion is immoral.
- We ought to protect Liu from the angry mob.
- My father is a good man.

Is Moral Reasoning Possible?

Some people claim that reasoning about morality is not possible because moral statements are not statements at all. This view is a moral theory known as emotivism. Emotivism says that moral statements are just not the kinds of things that can be true or false. They are more like exclamations such as "Hooray!" or "Bah!" They are expressions of emotion, not statements of fact. So according to emotivism, the sentence "Capital punishment is wrong" means something like "Capital punishment—boo!"

But this theory has been severely criticized by moral philosophers. They contend, for example, that in several ways the theory conflicts with our experience of the moral life. Our everyday moral experience seems to suggest that we sometimes have moral disagreements with others. The notion that we do have disagreements seems to most people like a simple matter of common sense. But according to emotivism, moral disagreements are impossible. Since moral utterances are not statements, they cannot contradict one another. If you say "ice cream—yes!" and someone else says "ice cream—yuk!" the two of you are not disagreeing; you're just venting. But our moral experience seems to show that in moral disagreements we are doing much more than expressing emotion. In addition, emotivism says that nothing is good or bad, right or wrong, because these terms don't refer to anything. But our moral experience appears to suggest that some things really are good or bad, right or wrong. Many moral philosophers believe that these considerations show that emotivism must be mistaken.

Critics who take this line of argument against emotivism admit that our commonsense moral experience may be misleading. It's possible that emotivism is correct after all. Commonsense views of the world have been wrong in the past. But, these critics assert, we are justified in believing what common sense tells us unless we have good reason to doubt it.

Moral statements are plainly different from nonmoral, or descriptive, statements. Nonmoral statements do not assert that something is right or wrong, good or bad—they simply describe a state of affairs without giving it a value one way or the other. Compare these nonmoral statements with the moral statements just given:

> A system of morality which is based on relative emotional values is a mere illusion, a thoroughly vulgar conception which has nothing sound in it and nothing true.
>
> —Socrates

- Serena did not keep her promise to you.
- James was treated harshly.
- Some people think abortion is immoral.
- Liu was protected from the angry mob.
- My father tried to be a good man.

The standard moral argument is a mixture of moral and nonmoral statements. At least one premise is a moral statement that asserts a general moral principle or moral standard. At least one premise makes a nonmoral claim. And the conclusion is a moral statement, or judgment, about a particular case (usually a particular kind of action). For example:

Argument 1

1. *It is wrong to inflict unnecessary pain on a child.*
2. *Spanking inflicts unnecessary pain on a child.*
3. *Therefore, spanking is wrong.*

In this simple argument, premise 1 is a moral statement, affirming a general moral principle. Premise 2 is a nonmoral statement describing the nature of a specific kind of action. And the conclusion is the moral statement that the argument is intended to establish. It is about a specific kind of action.

A standard moral argument has this form for good reason. In a moral argument, we simply cannot establish the conclusion (a moral statement) without a moral premise. A moral argu-

---

Further Thought

Moral and Nonmoral Statements

Is this a moral statement: "I am opposed to abortion"? How about this one: "I feel very strongly that abortion is wrong"? Actually in many contexts, statements like these are not meant to be moral statements at all; they are not meant to assert that an action is right or wrong or that a person is good or bad. They are used instead to report on someone's state of mind. Saying that you feel a certain way toward an action is not the same thing as stating that the action is wrong. But be careful. Sometimes statements like these really are meant as moral statements. Context will usually tell you which kind of statement is intended.

---

ment with only nonmoral premises does not work.

To put it another way, we cannot infer what *should be* or *ought to be* (in the conclusion) from statements about *what is*. Suppose the previous argument reads like this (and there are no missing premises):

> *Spanking inflicts unnecessary pain on a child.*
>
> *Therefore, spanking is wrong.*

The premise doesn't say anything about right or wrong; it just makes a descriptive claim. The conclusion, though, does assert something about right or wrong. So the conclusion is not supported by the premise; it does not follow from the descriptive statement.

Here's another example:

> *Torturing prisoners of war is a case of intentional mistreatment.*
>
> *Prisoners of war should not be tortured.*

This argument fails because the moral premise is missing. We need a moral premise to connect the nonmoral premise to the conclusion, like this:

Argument 2

No prisoner of war should ever be intentionally mistreated.

Torturing prisoners of war is a case of intentional mistreatment.

Prisoners of war should not be tortured.

Can't We All Just Get Along?

Despite the prevalence of moral disagreements on countless issues, there is a surprising amount of agreement on basic moral principles. Often, the bone of contention in moral arguments is not the moral premises (which may be widely accepted), but the nonmoral ones. In debates about "pulling the plug" on severely comatose patients, for example, all parties may agree that murder is wrong but disagree about the nature of comatose patients. Some may insist that comatose patients are entities that can be murdered (because they are fully human, true persons, etc.); others, that comatose patients are not the kind of entities that can be murdered (because they are not persons, for example). So there may not be as much moral disagreement in the world as you might think. Here's a list of moral principles that both parties in moral debates often accept:

- **Personal benefit:** Acknowledge the extent to which an action produces beneficial consequences for the individual in question.

- **Principle of benevolence:** Help those in need.

- **Principle of harm:** Do not harm others.

- **Principle of honesty:** Do not deceive others.

- **Principle of lawfulness:** Do not violate the law.

- **Principle of autonomy:** Acknowledge a person's freedom over his/her actions or physical body.

- **Principle of justice:** Acknowledge a person's right to due process, fair compensation for harm done, and fair distribution of benefits.

- **Rights:** Acknowledge a person's rights to life, information, privacy, free expression, and safety.

In the standard moral argument, we also need a nonmoral premise. Remember that the conclusion is a moral statement (judgment) about a particular kind of action. The moral premise, however, is a statement expressing a general moral principle about a much broader class of actions. In order to infer the narrower conclusion from a much broader premise, we need a nonmoral statement to bridge the gap. For example, from the general moral principle that "no prisoner of war should ever be intentionally mistreated," we cannot conclude that "prisoners of war should not be tortured" unless there is a nonmoral premise stating that torturing prisoners of war is a type of intentional mistreatment. Likewise from the general moral principle that "murder is wrong," we cannot conclude that "abortion is wrong" unless there's a factual premise telling us that abortion is murder.

Now, very often when you encounter moral arguments, they are abbreviated and missing the moral premise (the general moral principle), like the arguments discussed earlier:

Spanking inflicts unnecessary pain on a child.

Therefore, spanking is wrong.

Torturing prisoners of war is a case of intentional mistreatment.

Prisoners of war should not be tortured.

Usually, the moral premise is missing because it's implicit. In such cases, to make sense of the argument, you must supply the implicit premise. Sometimes you may automatically add the implicit premise in your head without bothering to properly fill out the argument. But if you want to carefully evaluate moral arguments, it's best to spell out any missing premises. Implicit moral premises are often dubious and need to be studied closely. General moral principles that are taken for granted may turn out to be unfounded or incomplete. Also, laying everything out on the table like this is essential if you want to improve the argument—an important exercise if you care that your positions on moral issues are well supported.

The simplest approach to identifying implicit premises is to treat moral arguments as deductive. (Notice that arguments 1 and 2 are valid deductive arguments.) Your task, then, is to supply plausible premises that will make the argument valid. . . . Consider this argument:

Cloning humans is unnatural.

Therefore, cloning humans is morally wrong.

As it stands, this argument is not valid, and we can see right away that the missing premise is a general moral principle. A plausible premise to make this argument valid, then, is "Anything unnatural is morally wrong," a general moral principle. The revised version is:

Argument 3

Anything unnatural is morally wrong.

Cloning humans is unnatural.

Therefore, cloning humans is morally wrong.

Here's another incomplete argument:

Meg lied to her sister for no good reason.

Therefore, Meg should not have lied to her sister.

To make this argument valid and to supply a general moral principle, we can add this premise:

Argument 4

One should not lie without good reason.

Meg lied to her sister for no good reason.

Therefore, Meg should not have lied to her sister.

> So, if we can support our [moral] judgments with good reasons, and provide explanations of why these reasons matter, and show that the case on the other side is weak, what more in the way of proof could anyone possibly want?
>
> —James Rachels

Another advantage to treating moral arguments as deductive (and to supplying explicit premises that will make the arguments valid) is ease of analysis. Generally, moral arguments are easier to appraise and modify when they are deductive. And if they are deductively valid, you know that any flaws in the arguments will likely be the result of false premises. For example, if you have a deductively valid argument, and the conclusion is false, you know that at least one of the premises is false.

Moral Premises

In good arguments the inferences are valid or strong and the premises—whether nonmoral or moral—are true. This latter stipulation means that to make good arguments, you must ensure that the premises are backed by good reasons and are not simply assumed without warrant. To evaluate arguments, you must check the premises for these same qualities. As noted in previous chapters, accurately assessing the truth of nonmoral premises depends mostly on your knowledge of the subject matter, including the results of relevant scientific research, the analyses of reliable experts, and the content of your background information. Gauging the truth of moral premises (moral principles) mostly involves examining the support they get from three sources: (1) other moral principles, (2) moral theories, and (3) considered moral judgments.

The appeal to another moral principle (usually a more general or higher-level principle) is probably the most common way to support a moral premise. Often the more general principle is extremely credible or accepted by all parties so that further support for it is unnecessary. Sometimes it is controversial so that it too is in need of support. Suppose the moral premise in question is, "A dying patient in intolerable and untreatable pain should be allowed to commit suicide with a physician's help." Some would say that this claim is derived from, or is based on, the higher (and more widely accepted) principle of autonomy—the notion that a person has an inherent right of self-determination, a right to make autonomous choices about his or her own life and death. Others would support the premise by appealing to the principle of beneficence, or mercy: If we are in a position to relieve the severe suffering of another without excessive cost to ourselves, we have a duty to do so. They would interpret this principle as sanctioning the physician's role in helping a competent, hopelessly ill patient to die. To try to show that the premise is false, someone might appeal to a sanctity-of-life principle, asserting that human life is sacred and should be preserved at all costs. When such higher principles are brought in, the truth of the original premise often becomes clear—or not. They cannot be the court of final appeal in ethics, for they too can be tested by reasoned argument showing why they should or should not be believed.

Reasons for accepting or rejecting a moral premise can also come from a moral theory, a general explanation of what makes an action right or what makes a person or motive good (see the next section). For example, traditional utilitarianism is a moral theory asserting that right actions are those that produce the greatest happiness for all concerned. To support the assisted suicide premise, you could appeal to the theory, arguing that the least amount of unhappiness (pain and suffering) for all concerned (patient, physician, and family) would result if the physician helped the patient die. To counter your argument, someone would need to show that your happiness calculations were incorrect (for example, that assisted suicide actually causes more unhappiness in the long run), or that utilitarianism itself is an inadequate theory, or that other theories or considerations are more important or relevant than utilitarian factors.

A moral premise can also be supported or undermined by our *considered moral judgments*. These are moral judgments that we consider credible after we carefully and dispassionately reflect on them. Pertaining to either specific cases or general statements, they constitute what philosophers have called our moral common sense. They are not infallible guides to morality, but unless we have good reasons for doubting their soundness, we are entitled to trust them. Some of our considered judgments may seem undeniable, even self-evident—for example: "Inflicting unnecessary, undeserved suffering on someone is wrong"; "Torturing children for the fun of it is immoral"; "Treating people harshly merely because of the color of their skin is unjust."

Moral principles, theories, and judgments relate to one another in interesting ways (a topic we explore in the following pages). For now, it's enough to note that we can evaluate moral premises by seeing if they conflict with principles, theories, or judgments that we have good reason to trust. Specifically, we can assess a moral premise the same way we might assess any other kind of universal generalization—by trying to think of counterexamples to it. Consider this deductively valid argument, a modified version of argument 3:

Argument 5

1. *The medical cloning of humans is unnatural because it is something that would not occur without human intervention.*

2. *All actions that are unnatural and that are not done for religious reasons should not be done.*

3. *The medical cloning of humans is never done for religious reasons.*

4. *Therefore, cloning humans should not be done.*

Premise 2 is the general moral principle here. Is it true? At the very least it is questionable. We know that it's questionable because we can think of counterexamples to it. That is, we can think of instances in which the principle seems not to hold. For example, what about the use of antibiotics to treat infections? The use of antibiotics is unnatural as defined in the argument (they are a good example of human intervention in the natural course of illness), and few would claim that antibiotics are employed for religious reasons. (The term "for religious reasons" is vague, but we will assume for the sake of this example that it means something like "as an integral part of established religious practice.") But despite its unnaturalness, the use of antibiotics seems to be morally acceptable to almost everyone. At any rate, it is difficult to imagine what a plausible argument against antibiotics would be like. So premise 2 appears to be false. We could probably refute premise 2 by using many other counterexamples, such as wearing clothes, drinking bottled water, and riding a bicycle.

Moral Theories

Very often when we assess moral arguments and in other ways think critically about morality, we are trying to come to a moral judgment about a particular issue or kind of action. We deliberate because we want to understand what's right or wrong, good or bad. Our moral judgments may appear as premises or conclusions in our arguments or as sturdy pillars of our moral common sense. They may be justified by appeals to general moral principles, which in turn may gain credibility from the most reliable of our moral judgments. But what of moral theories? In the previous section we saw how a moral theory can strengthen or weaken a moral premise. Yet that's only part of the story.

As we have seen, theories of morality are attempts to explain what makes an action right or what makes a person or motive good. They try to specify what all right actions and all good things have in common. As such, they can give support, guidance, or validation to our moral decision making, shaping our moral principles, judgments, and arguments. Traditional utilitarianism (mentioned earlier) is a well-known example of a moral theory. Another is the divine command theory, the view that what makes an action right is that God commands it or wills it. Ethical egoism asserts that right actions are those that promote one's own best interests.

Interestingly enough, we all have a moral theory. Whether we articulate it or not, we all have some kind of view of what makes actions right or persons good. Even the notion that there is no such thing as right or wrong is a moral theory. Even the idea that all moral theories are worthless or that all moral judgments are subjective, objective, relative, or meaningless is a moral theory. The critical question, then, is not whether you have a moral theory but whether the theory you have is a good one.

Moral theorizing is a fact of the moral life. We do moral theorizing when we ponder what rightness or goodness means, or try to furnish basic justification for a moral standard, or resolve a conflict between principles, or gauge the credibility of moral intuitions, or explain why an action is right or wrong. To theorize is to step back from the specifics of a case and try to see the larger pattern that can help us make sense of it all.

Despite the importance of moral theories, they are not the ultimate authority or sole referee in moral reasoning. A theory gives us very general norms, but morality is about more than just generalities— it's also about the particulars of individual moral judgments. How do the general and the particular fit together?

Here is one way. Suppose you must decide whether an action is morally permissible. From a plausible moral theory, you draw general guidance in the form of moral principles that apply to the case. If the principles appear to sanction conflicting decisions, you turn again to the theory for understanding in how to resolve the inconsistency. At the same time you consult your considered moral judgments. If your theory and your considered judgments lead you to the same conclusion, you have good reason to believe that the conclusion is correct. If your theory and considered judgments diverge, you must decide which is more credible. If the implications of your theory seem more plausible, you may decide to revise your considered judgments to cohere better with the theory. If your judgments seem more plausible, you may decide to alter your theory accordingly. If your credible judgments conflict drastically with your theory, you may be justified in giving up the theory altogether.

> In my view moral theorizing is something that real people do in everyday life. It is not just the domain of professors, expounding in their lecture halls. Moral theorizing can be found on the highways and byways, practiced by everyone from bartenders to politicians.
>
> —Dale Jamieson

Evaluating Moral Theories

As you may have gathered, several moral theories vie for our allegiance, each one with a distinctive take on morality and with different implications for moral issues. Moral philosophers remind us that theories also differ in quality: All moral theories are not created equal. Some theories are better than others. This fact immediately prompts two questions: Which moral theory is best, and how can we judge that it is the best? . . . To identify the best theory, we must compare competing theories and use the criteria of adequacy to appraise their worth. The criteria of adequacy that we use in judging moral theories are a little different from those we use to assess other types of theories, though the two sets of criteria have much in common. In significant ways, too, moral theories are much like scientific theories, and the process of theory evaluation is similar in both cases.

How are moral theories like scientific theories? Recall that scientific theories try to explain the causes of events, everything from tumor growth to exploding stars. A plausible scientific theory is one that's consistent with all the relevant data. A theory explaining the cause of a fatal illness, for example, must take into account facts about patient symptoms, medical test results, medical histories, environmental factors, and more. Moral theories, on the other hand, try to explain what makes an action right or what makes a person good. A plausible moral theory must also be consistent with the relevant data. The data that moral theories try to explain are our considered moral judgments, the moral judgments we accept after we reason about them carefully. Any plausible moral theory must be consistent with those

Critiquing Moral Theories

Most moral philosophers don't buy the idea that one moral theory is as good as any other. They spend a good deal of time evaluating moral theories to gauge their worth, and some theories don't fare very well under this scrutiny. Here, for example, are some typical criticisms of three controversial moral theories.

SUBJECTIVE RELATIVISM

This view states that what makes an action right for someone is that it is approved by that person. Moral judgments are relative to what each person believes. If you say that stealing is wrong, then it's wrong (for you). If someone else says that stealing is right, then it's right (for her). Moral philosophers, though, think that the theory has several problematic implications. For example, the theory implies that each person is morally infallible. If you truly approve of an action, then it's right, and you cannot be wrong. Subjective relativism also makes moral disagreement nearly impossible. You disagree with others when you think they are mistaken. But according to subjective relativism, no one could be mistaken. These and other implications, critics say, render the theory implausible.

CULTURAL RELATIVISM

This view claims that what makes an action right is that it's approved by one's culture. If your culture deems something to be right, it's right. Moral truth is relative to cultures. As you might expect, this view is criticized for many of the same problems that plague subjective relativism. It implies that cultures are infallible. This means that if most people living in Nazi Germany during World War II had approved of the extermination of The Jews, then the Holocaust was morally right. It seems, though, that societies are no more infallible than individuals are. What's more, cultural relativism implies that it would be impossible to disagree with one's culture and be right. Social reformers such as Martin Luther King, Jr., or Gandhi could not claim that an action approved by society is wrong, for if society approves of it, the action is right. For these and other reasons, most moral philosophers view cultural relativism as a questionable moral theory.

ETHICAL EGOISM

In this view, what makes an action right is that it promotes one's own best interests. It doesn't imply that you should do anything you want because, in the long run, that may not be in your own best interest. Ethical egoism could even condone altruism on the grounds that being nice to other people is in your best interest. Critics, however, say that the theory is implausible because it sanctions all sorts of abominable acts. For example, if it's in your best interest to kill your boss, and if you could do it without suffering any negative consequences (such as getting caught), then ethical egoism says that your moral duty is to kill him.

considered moral judgments. As we have seen, they are fallible and revisable, but we are entitled to believe them unless we have good reason to doubt them. If a moral theory is seriously inconsistent with them—if, for example, it approves of obviously immoral acts (such as inflicting pain on innocent children for no good reason or treating equals unequally)—it is dubious, perhaps even fatally flawed, and deserving of radical revision or rejection. So the first criterion of adequacy for moral theories is: *consistency with considered moral judgments.*

In science (and many other fields of inquiry) there is an interesting relationship between theory and data. The data have an impact on the theory because the theory explains the data. A good theory, on the other hand, can lead scientists to reject certain data. Scientists want the data and theory to match up as closely as possible. They want the match to be so close that significant changes in either the data or theory aren't necessary. Moral theories work this way too. As suggested earlier, our moral data (our considered moral judgments) influence our moral theory. And our moral theory can lead us to accept or reject certain data. Ideally, we want the fit between data and theory to be as close as possible. In other words, we want to achieve what moral philosophers refer to as a "reflective equilibrium" between facts and theory. We want the fit to be so close that significant adjustments in either data or theory are not necessary.

In addition to being consistent with the data, a plausible scientific theory must also be conservative. It must be consistent with background information—that is, with well-founded beliefs such as reliable scientific findings and well-established theories. Plausible moral theories must also be consistent with the relevant background information—that is, with our experience of the moral life. Whatever else our moral experience involves, it certainly includes (1) making moral judgments (we do this constantly), (2) having moral disagreements (we occasionally do this), and (3) sometimes acting immorally (we recognize that we are not morally perfect). If a moral theory suggests that we do not have these experiences, we must view the theory with suspicion. Another criterion of adequacy for moral theories, then, is *consistency with our experience of the moral life*.

Now, it's possible that our experience of the moral life is an illusion, only seeming to involve making moral judgments, having moral disagreements, and getting into moral disagreements. But unless we have good reason to believe that our moral experience is an illusion, we are justified in accepting it at face value.

A scientific theory gains in credibility if it helps to solve problems (has fruitfulness and scope). A plausible moral theory must also help to solve problems. That is, it must help us make moral decisions, especially those that involve moral dilemmas, instances where moral principles or moral judgments are in conflict. After all, the reason we want a moral theory is that it helps guide our actions and reconcile clashing moral beliefs. A moral theory that offers no help with such moral problems is said to be *unworkable*. Unworkable moral theories are inferior. So a final criterion of adequacy for moral theories is *workability in real-life situations*.

Review Notes

Moral Criteria of Adequacy

1. Consistency with our considered moral judgments

2. Consistency with our experience of the moral life

3. Workability in real-life situations

Now let's see how we can use these criteria to take the measure of two fundamentally different theories: traditional utilitarianism and Kantian ethics.

Traditional utilitarianism was founded by Jeremy Bentham (1748–1832) and later refined by John Stuart Mill (1806–1873). Bentham's idea was that right actions are those that achieve the greatest happiness for the greatest number. He declared that by this simple standard all actions could be judged. Many people embraced the theory, for it seemed so much more rational than moral theories of the time, which often rested on dubious assumptions. In the nineteenth century, traditional utilitarianism inspired reformers who worked to abolish slavery, eliminate child labor, and increase recognition of women's rights.

To be more precise, traditional utilitarianism says that what makes an action right is that it maximizes overall happiness, everyone considered. Acting morally in any given situation, then, involves calculating how much happiness can be produced by several possible actions, identifying the persons who will be affected by those actions, and opting for the one action that produces the greatest amount of happiness in the world. Notice that what matters in utilitarianism is the *consequences* of an action—not whether the action breaks a rule or violates some abstract principle. If happiness is maximized by a particular action, then the action is morally right, regardless of any other considerations. By the lights of utilitarianism, the end justifies the means.

How does traditional utilitarianism fare when judged by the moral criteria of adequacy? For starters, the theory does seem to be consistent with key aspects of our experience of the moral life. The theory assumes that we can and do make moral judgments, have moral disagreements, and act immorally.

Some critics, however, have questioned whether traditional utilitarianism is a workable theory because calculating amounts of happiness seems to be extremely difficult or impossible. For example, each action we perform has consequences indefinitely into the future. If this is the case, then at what point should we make our calculation of the happiness produced? Should we figure into our calculations the happiness that will accrue by next Tuesday? next year? next decade? Some actions may produce very little happiness in the short run but a great deal of happiness over the long haul. Some actions work the other way round— big short-term benefits, no long-term payback. Traditional utilitarianism offers no help in resolving this problem, and so critics have accused the theory of being unworkable.

Many moral philosophers think that the theory faces a much bigger problem than unworkability: It seems to conflict with many of our considered moral judgments. For instance, the theory seems inconsistent with our considered moral judgments involving rights. We tend to think that certain things should not be done to people even if doing them would produce the greatest amount of happiness in the world. We would not think it right to falsely accuse and punish an innocent person just because doing so would make a whole town of people happy. We would not think it right to torture one person just because the action would make a dozen other people extremely happy. Our considered moral judgments say that such actions are wrong, but traditional utilitarianism says they may be right.

Suppose two possible actions will produce exactly the same amount of overall happiness. But one of the actions involves the violation of someone's rights or causes a serious injustice. According to utilitarianism, the two actions are equally right. But to many, this evaluation of the situation seems to conflict with our considered moral judgments.

The same kind of conflict arises in regard to moral duties. Most of us believe that we have certain duties to other people that often seem more weighty than considerations of

In recent years, stories like this one have been appearing in the news with shocking frequency:

Fawaz later recalled that his wife, Zahra, was sleeping soundly on her side and curled slightly against the pillow when he rose at dawn and readied himself for work at his construction job on the outskirts of Damascus. It was a rainy Sunday morning in January and very cold; as he left, Fawaz turned back one last time to tuck the blanket more snugly around his 16-year-old wife. Zahra slept on without stirring, and her husband locked the door of their tiny apartment carefully behind him.

Zahra was most likely still sleeping when her older brother, Fayyez, entered the apartment a short time later, using a stolen key and carrying a dagger. His sister lay on the carpeted floor, on the thin, foam mattress she shared with her husband, so Fayyez must have had to kneel next to Zahra as he raised the dagger and stabbed her five times in the head and back: brutal, tearing thrusts that shattered the base of her skull and nearly severed her spinal column. Leaving the door open, Fayyez walked downstairs and out to the local police station. There, he reportedly turned himself in, telling the officers on duty that he had killed his sister in order to remove the dishonor she had brought on the family by losing her virginity out of wedlock nearly 10 months earlier.

"Fayyez told the police, 'It is my right to correct this error,'" Maha Ali, a Syrian lawyer who knew Zahra and now works pro bono for her husband, told me not long ago. "He said, 'It's true that my sister is married now, but we never washed away the shame.'"

Fayyez had committed an honor killing, a murder for the sake of a family's honor, usually involving the slaying of a sister, wife, or daughter thought to have disgraced the family by immoral behavior. Nowadays women are killed for having an extramarital affair, having premarital sex, being flirtatious, being raped or sexually abused, or otherwise violating some cultural taboo. The United Nations Population Fund estimates that each year about 5000 honor killings are committed in countries all over the globe. They have occurred in the United States, Europe, Africa, and the Middle East, mostly in Muslim communities where they are generally approved of or at least tolerated to some degree.

Honor killings have presented a disquieting challenge to Western cultural relativists, who are committed to saying that the murders are morally permissible if they are approved by the culture involved. But this view often conflicts with that of the relativists' own culture, which may endorse universal human rights (including women's rights) and strongly condemn such murders.

Do you believe that honor killings are wrong—even in those cultures that approve of them? On what grounds? If you are a relativist, are you a consistent one, conceding that honor killings are right if one's culture sanctions them? If you think they are objectively wrong, do you also judge other heinous acts wrong even though they are culturally sanctioned?

happiness. For example, we believe that in general we have a duty to keep our promises to people. But traditional utilitarianism does not recognize any such duties. It says that our only goal should be to maximize happiness—regardless of whether we have to break a promise to do it.

So for these reasons (and a few others), many critics have accused the theory of being acutely inconsistent with relevant moral data. They believe that any theory that runs afoul of the criterion of consistency in this way cannot be correct.

But take note: Even the fiercest critics of utilitarianism have admitted that the theory does seem to capture something essential to moral theories—the notion that the consequences of actions are indeed relevant to moral judgments. Probably very few people would want to say that in moral decision making the consequences of their actions never matter.

For the record, the sketch of traditional utilitarianism given here has been oversimplified so we can focus on the process of theory assessment. Over the years, utilitarians have modified the theory to make it more plausible. Critics, however, still claim that the theory is flawed . . . but that's another story.

In radical contrast to utilitarianism and other theories basing rghtness on the consequences of actions, the moral theory of Immanuel Kant (1724–1804) says that rightness does not depend at all on the production of happiness or on the satisfaction of human desires. For Kant, rightness is not defined by an action's results, but by its form—that is, by the nature of the action itself. Harming the innocent is wrong not because it causes unhappiness, but because of the kind of action it is. Morality is about conforming your actions to universal moral rules derived from reason and doing so for duty's sake alone. Your actions are right only if they are consistent with such rules, and you deserve praise for right actions only if you act solely from a sense of duty.

In Kantian ethics, the moral rules (or duties) are expressed as categorical imperatives—that is, as commands that apply without exception (categorically, or absolutely) and without regard to a person's preferences or goals. Kant says that we can infer all our duties from one moral principle, the ultimate categorical imperative. He formulates it in several ways but supposes that they are all equivalent. His first formulation says, "Act only on that maxim through which you can at the same time will that it should become a universal law." On Kant's view, our actions imply general moral rules, or maxims. To tell a lie for personal gain is essentially to act according to a maxim that says something like, "It's morally permissible to lie to someone to promote your own interests." To determine if an action is permissible, we need to ask ourselves if we could consistently will that the maxim of our action become a universal moral law that applies to everyone. We must ask, "Could all humankind, with logical consistency, act on the maxim, and would we be willing to have them do that?" If the answer is yes on both counts, the action is morally permissible; if not, it is prohibited.

Here is Kant's illustration of properly applying this formulation. Suppose that to borrow money from a friend (money that you know you will never pay back), you falsely promise to repay the loan. Is this behavior permissible? To find out, you must ask if you could consistently will that the maxim of your action become a universal law. The maxim of your action is, "Whenever you need money that you know you cannot pay back, make a lying promise to obtain the loan." What would happen if everyone acted according to this maxim? Everyone would make lying promises to get a loan, but everyone would also know that the promises were empty—and the practice of loaning money based on a promise would cease to exist. The result is a contradiction: The universal making of lying promises would end the practice of promising. Thus you cannot consistently will that the maxim of your action become a universal law, so making a lying promise to borrow money is prohibited.

This bare sketch of only one formulation of the categorical imperative does not do justice to Kant's theory, but it's enough for an illustration of how we might apply the moral criteria of adequacy.

One fact that seems obvious is that the theory easily passes the second criterion: It is generally consistent with our experience of the moral life. According to Kantian ethics, we do form moral judgments, have moral disagreements, and err in our moral beliefs. Any flaws in the theory are more likely to arise from the first criterion; sure enough, critics insist that the theory is not consistent with our considered moral judgments. One argument for this conclusion starts from Kant's claim that the moral rules are absolute—that is, they must be obeyed without exception (or as he says, we have "perfect" duties). He asserts, for example, that we have an absolute duty not to lie or to kill the innocent, regardless of the consequences of observing the rule. Suppose a crazed killer wants to murder an innocent man who takes refuge in your house. The killer knocks at your door and asks you if the man is hiding inside. If you tell the truth, the innocent man will be murdered; if you lie, he will be saved. What would Kant have you do in a case like this? His answer is unequivocal: You must tell the truth though it leads to the murder of an innocent person. How does this absolutism fit with our moral common sense? Not very well, critics say. Our considered moral judgments seem to suggest that, in general, saving an innocent life has far more moral value than blindly adhering to an absolute rule. Moral common sense seems to affirm that doing our duty for duty's sake—though generally a worthy aim—is sometimes less important than avoiding tragic consequences. Kant would have us do our duty though the heavens fall, but that view appears inconsistent with moral judgments that we have good reasons to trust.

Given enough space, we could review the responses that Kant's defenders have offered to this criticism (and to others). And we could dwell on the formulation of the categorical imperative that some consider Kant's greatest insight—the principle of respect for persons. But this brief treatment will have to do.

Between utilitarianism and Kantian ethics, which theory is better and why? An adequate answer to that question would be anything but brief. Comparing the virtues and vices of these two theories, and then deciding which one is preferable, would require a great deal of careful analysis and critical thinking. But however the task proceeds, it is sure to involve applying to both theories some telling criteria of adequacy (either the three criteria discussed here, or variations on them, and perhaps others). Such an investigation would show that neither theory is perfect (no theory is) and would likely yield an edifying conclusion such as (1) one theory is more plausible than the other, or (2) both theories are seriously defective, or (3) the best elements of both can be blended into a new theory, or (4) one of the theories is an especially good candidate for modification to eliminate shortcomings.

Applying the criteria is not like solving a mathematical equation or following a set of instructions to build a gasoline engine. There is no rigid rubric for using or weighting the criteria to sort good theories from bad. But like the scientific criteria of adequacy, these standards do give us guidance in making reasonable judgments about the objective strengths and weaknesses of theories.

• • •

A Coherent Worldview

Making a coherent and powerful worldview for yourself is the work of a lifetime, requiring reflection, critical thinking, and (often) personal anguish. So there is no way that this chapter—or *any* chapter, book, or person—can provide you with ready-made content for your worldview. But we can trace out some characteristics that any good worldview should possess.

A worldview is a massive intellectual construct with many elements. We can get a handle on it, though, by thinking of it as primarily a composite of theories—theories about morality, God, science, mind, personhood, society, knowledge, and much more. We all have our own beliefs about these things, and our most general beliefs often congeal into theories. Since worldviews are framed out of theories, good worldviews will, as a minimum requirement, consist of good theories. So much of the job of devising a good worldview consists of ensuring that our theories are the best theoretical explanations available. We do that, of course, by putting our theories to the test as we have in previous chapters.

But there's more to crafting a plausible worldview than that. . . . When some of our most fundamental beliefs conflict with one another, the relevant theory is in trouble and our understanding is decreased. After all, if two of our beliefs are inconsistent with one another, we know that at least one of them must be false. To achieve true understanding, we must somehow resolve the inconsistency. Likewise, if the theories that make up our worldview are inconsistent with one another, there is obviously something wrong with our worldview. At least one of our theories must be flawed, and some of our beliefs must be wrong. Our understanding of the world is decreased, and our prospects for success (however we define it) are dimmed. A crucial criterion, then, for judging a worldview is *internal consistency*—the requirement that the theories composing our worldview do not conflict.

How can our best theories conflict? Here are some ways:

- *Our moral theory can conflict with our view of human freedom.* Most people believe that persons can be held morally responsible for their actions—as long as they act freely. That is, persons can be praised or blamed only for those actions over which they have control. But many people also think that humans cannot act freely, that they do not have free will. They believe in causal determinism, the view that every event in the universe has a cause (is determined). This means that everything that happens (including human actions) has a preceding cause, so that the chain of causes stretches back into the indefinite past—out of our control. Many would see this situation as an unacceptable conflict between their moral theory and their view of the way the world is.

- *Our theory about the existence of God can conflict with our scientific theory about the nature of the universe.* Some people argue that God must exist because everything has a cause, including the universe, and the only thing that could have caused the universe is God. Modern physics, however, shows that some things in the universe (namely, certain subatomic particles) often occur uncaused, so it's not true that everything has a cause. Thus, in this instance science seems to be at odds with a certain brand of theology.

- *Our theory about the mind can be in conflict with theories of personal survival after death.* Some believe that people can live on in some ethereal form (as souls or disembodied minds, for example) after death. This notion accords well with the idea that the mind (our true essence) is the kind of thing that can exist independently of the body. But this kind of survival after death would not be possible if the mind is identical to the body, as some people believe.

The work of building plausible worldviews will always involve eliminating inconsistencies. If you really want to understand the world and your place in it, you must wrestle with these inconsistencies. Reconciling conflicting beliefs (by eliminating them or modifying them) is a necessary condition for creating theories and a worldview that can successfully guide your thinking, your choices, and your deeds.

With this discussion, we now come full circle to a theme that bubbles up in the first few pages of this book and flows through each chapter to this final paragraph: Every statement, every theory, and every worldview is fair game for critical thinking. No claim can be considered immune to critical inquiry, revision, and rejection. We will probably never be able to evaluate the truth of all our beliefs, but we violate the spirit of critical reasoning and do ourselves a disfavor if we cordon them off and post a sign that says "Off Limits!" If truth is what we seek, if knowledge is our goal, we should be willing to turn the light of critical thinking on any dark corner anywhere. This point is especially relevant to the development of worldviews, which too often are thought to be the unalterable givens of clan and culture, ideologies carved in the pillars of the mind forever. Our worldviews are far too important not to subject them to intelligent, reasoned reflection.

Key Words

moral statement   worldview

Summary

Moral Arguments

- A moral argument is an argument in which the conclusion is a moral statement. A moral statement is a statement asserting that an action is right or wrong (moral or immoral) or that a person or motive is good or bad.

- In a moral argument, we cannot establish the conclusion without a moral premise. A standard moral argument has at least one premise that asserts a general moral principle, at least one premise that is a nonmoral claim, and a conclusion that is a moral statement.

- Often a moral premise in a moral argument is implicit. The best approach to identifying the implicit premises is to treat moral arguments as deductive. Your job then is to supply plausible premises that will make the argument valid.

Moral Premises

- Gauging the truth of moral premises (moral principles) mostly involves examining the support they get from three sources: (1) other moral principles, (2) moral theories, and (3) considered moral judgments.
- We can assess the truth of a moral premise the same way we might assess any other kind of universal generalization—by trying to think of counterexamples to it.

Moral Theories

- Theories of morality are attempts to explain what makes an action right or what makes a person good. We test moral theories the same way we test any other theory—by applying criteria of adequacy to a theory and its competitors.
- The criteria of adequacy for moral theories are (1) consistency with considered moral judgments, (2) consistency with our experience of the moral life, and (3) workability in real-life situations.

Coherent Worldview

- Worldviews are composites of theories, including theories of morality. A good worldview must consist of good theories. But it also must have internal consistency—the theories composing our worldview must not conflict.
- Our worldviews are far too important not to subject them to intelligent, reasoned reflection.

EXERCISES

Exercise 4.1

REVIEW QUESTIONS

1. What is a moral theory?
2. According to the text, what is a worldview?
3. What is a moral statement?
4. What is the basic structure of a standard moral argument?
5. Why can't we infer a moral statement from nonmoral statements alone?
6. Why is it important to spell out implicit premises in a moral argument?
7. What technique can we use to determine whether a general moral principle is true?
8. What is a moral judgment?
9. According to the text, what precisely does a moral theory try to explain?

10. According to the text, what are the criteria of adequacy for appraising moral theories?

11. According to the text, how are moral theories like scientific theories?

12. Who founded the moral theory known as traditional utilitarianism?

13. According to the text, what is a crucial criterion for judging a worldview?

14. How do judges use analogical argument in deciding cases?

15. Why can't judges use deductive reasoning alone in their deliberations?

Exercise 4.2

Specify whether the following statements are moral or nonmoral.

1. Joan worries whether she's doing the right thing.

2. When the government restricts freedom of the press, it harms every citizen.

3. The government should not restrict freedom of the press.

4. Paul was sure that he saw Gregory steal the book from the library.

5. Because of the terrible results of the bombing, it's clear that the entire war effort was immoral.

6. The Church should never have allowed pedophile priests to stay in the priesthood.

7. The officer was justified in using deadly force because his life was threatened.

8. The officer used deadly force because his life was threatened.

9. Lying is wrong unless the lie involves trivial matters.

10. The officials should never have allowed the abuse to continue.

Exercise 4.3

In each of the following passages, add a moral premise to turn it into a valid moral argument.

1. Noah promised to drive Thelma to Los Angeles, so he should stop bellyaching and do it.

2. The refugees were shot at and lied to, and the authorities did nothing to stop any of this. The authorities should have intervened.

3. There was never any imminent threat from the Iraqi government, so the United States should not have invaded Iraq.

4. The Indian government posed an imminent threat to Pakistan and the world, so the Pakistanis were justified in attacking Indian troops.

5. Burton used a gun in the commission of a crime; therefore he should get a long prison term.

6. Ellen knew that a murder was going to take place. It was her duty to try to stop it.

7. Ahmed should never have allowed his daughter to receive in vitro fertilization. Such a procedure is unnatural.

8. The doctors performed the experiment on twenty patients without their consent. Obviously, that was wrong.

9. What you did was immoral. You hacked into a database containing personal information on thousands of people and invaded their privacy.

10. Ling spent all day weeding Mrs. Black's garden for no pay. The least Mrs. Black should do is let Ling borrow some gardening tools.

Exercise 4.4

Use counterexamples to test each of the following general moral principles.

1. Anything that is unnatural is immoral.

2. It is always and everywhere wrong to tell a lie.

3. In all circumstances the killing of a human being is wrong.

4. In all situations in which our actions can contribute to the welfare, safety, or happiness of others, we should treat all persons equally.

5. Any action that serves one's own best interests is morally permissible.

6. Any action that is approved of by one's society is moral.

7. Assisted suicide is never morally justified.

8. Whatever action a person approves of is morally right.

9. Making a promise to someone incurs a moral obligation to keep the promise in all circumstances.

10. Any action done for religious reasons is morally acceptable because religious reasons carry more weight than secular ones.

Exercise 4.5

Identify the moral argument in each of the following passages. Specify the premises and the conclusion, adding implicit premises where needed.

1. The movie *Lorenzo's Oil* is about a family's struggle to find a cure for their young son's fatal genetic disease, an illness that usually kills boys before they reach their eleventh birthday. The script is based on the true story of a family's attempt to save Lorenzo, their son, from this fatal genetic disease through the use of a medicinal oil. The movie is a tear-jerker, but it ends on a hopeful note that suggests that the oil will eventually cure Lorenzo and that the oil is an effective treatment for the genetic disease. The problem is, there is no cure for the disease and no good scientific evidence showing that the oil works. But the movie touts the oil anyway— and gives false hope to every family whose son suffers from this terrible illness. Worse, the movie overplays the worth of the oil, seriously misleading people about the medical facts. The movie, therefore, is immoral. It violates the ageless moral dictum to, above all else, "do no harm." *Lorenzo's Oil* may be just a movie, but it has done harm nonetheless.

2. "I, like many of my fellow Muslims, was appalled by the latest bombings in Saudi Arabia ('Among the Saudis, Attack Has Soured Qaeda Supporters' front page, Nov. 11). Yet I was disturbed to get the sense that Saudis were angered by this latest act of barbarity because the targets were mainly Arab and Muslim.

   "You quote one person as saying of the bombing in Riyadh in May, 'At that time it was seen as justifiable because there was an invasion of a foreign country, there was frustration.' Another says, 'Jihad is not against your own people.'

   "Regardless of whether the victims are Muslim or not, the vicious murder of innocent human beings is reprehensible and repugnant, an affront to everything Islam stands for. Any sympathy for Al Qaeda among the minority of Saudis should have evaporated after the May bombings in Riyadh, and it should have surprised no one in Saudi Arabia that Al Qaeda would attack a housing complex full of Arabs and Muslims.

   "That is what Al Qaeda is: a band of bloodthirsty murderers." [Letter to the editor, *New York Times*]

3. John and Nancy Jones had a two-year-old son who suffered from a serious but very curable bowel obstruction. For religious reasons, the Joneses decided to treat their son with prayer instead of modern medicine. They refused medical treatment even though they were told by several doctors that the child would die unless medically treated. As it turned out, the boy did

die. The Joneses were arrested and charged with involuntary manslaughter. Were the Joneses wrong to refuse treatment for their son? The answer is yes. Regardless of what faith or religious dogma would have the Joneses do, they allowed their child to die. According to just about any moral outlook, the care of a child by the parents is a fundamental obligation. Above all other concerns, parents have a duty to ensure the health and safety of their children and to use whatever means are most likely to secure those benefits. The Joneses ignored this basic moral principle. They were wrong—and deserve whatever punishment the state deems appropriate.

Exercise 4.6

Read the following description of a moral theory and answer the questions that follow.

The Ethics of Love Theory

According to the Ethics of Love Theory, what makes an action right is that it is based on love toward others. Love is the only universal moral good. In any situation where a moral choice must be made, this theory says that we must ask ourselves: "Which action would demonstrate the greatest degree of love for others, everyone considered?" So in this theory, actions that demonstrate love (such as respecting others, telling the truth, treating people equally, caring for them, protecting them from harm) would always be preferred over actions that do not demonstrate love (discriminating against persons, lying to them, harming them, stealing from them, ignoring them if they ask for help). Also, actions that demonstrate great love (such as risking your life to save theirs) would be preferred over those that exhibit only small degrees of love (such as being courteous).

1. Is this theory consistent with our considered moral judgments? Is it consistent with our judgments regarding the punishment of criminals? acts of war? providing for one's family as opposed to providing for all persons equally? If the theory conflicts with our considered moral judgments, provide an example demonstrating the conflict.

2. Is this theory consistent with our experience of the moral life? According to this theory, are moral judgments possible? Can we have moral disagreements? Can we ever act immorally?

3. Is this theory workable? Does it help you make moral decisions in these situations?

   a. Your beloved mother has a terminal illness which causes her unimaginable pain, and she begs you to kill her.

   b. You promise to buy your beloved spouse a car, but a half dozen homeless people beg you to give them the money that you had set aside for the car.

   c. You are a doctor who must decide which of one hundred patients should receive a life-saving organ transplant. You can choose only one, though you love all of them. Some are elderly; some, in great pain; some, very young; and some, Nobel laureates.

4. What is your final assessment of the ethics of love theory? Is it a good theory? Is it a better theory than traditional utilitarianism?

Chapter 5: Essays for Evaluation

Essay 1
Death Penalty Discriminates against Black Crime Victims

USA Today

April 29, 2003

Death penalty opponents have long complained that minorities are more likely to be executed than whites convicted of the same crime. Now a new study points up another troubling racial difference between who lives and who dies: the color of the victim.

While blacks and whites are murdered in roughly equal numbers in the USA, the killers of white people are six times as likely to be put to death, according to a statistical analysis released last week by the anti-death penalty human rights organization Amnesty International USA. It found that of 845 people executed since the U.S. resumed capital punishment in 1977, 80% were put to death for killing whites, while only 13% were executed for killing blacks.

The findings point to one chilling conclusion: The criminal justice system places a higher value on the lives of whites than on the lives of blacks and other minorities. That means minorities who are victims of violent crimes are also victimized by a legal system that fails to provide them the "equal protection of the laws" they are guaranteed under the 14th Amendment to the Constitution.

The report adds to the troubling evidence of racial discrimination against minority victims that has surfaced in other, state-level studies over the past year:

- In Illinois, juries have been three times as likely to sentence a person to death if the victim is white rather than black. Then-Gov. George Ryan cited those findings in January, when he commuted 167 death sentences to life imprisonment.

- In Maryland, the death penalty is four times as likely to be imposed when the victim is white rather than black. But a moratorium on executions imposed by the outgoing governor has been revoked by his successor.

Other studies in New Jersey, North Carolina, Pennsylvania, Texas and Virginia have shown similar results, as did a review a decade ago by the U.S. General Accounting Office, the investigative arm of Congress.

Other research suggests race-based differences in administering justice are not unique to the death penalty. A major study published by Stanford University in 1995 found that prosecutors tended to stereotype nonwhite crime victims as less-convincing witnesses, and cases involving nonwhite victims were more likely to be dismissed or result in plea-bargains to lesser penalties.

The Supreme Court banned the death penalty in 1972 after finding it was imposed arbitrarily. Five years later executions resumed based on the court's 1976 ruling that new laws would guide judges and juries to mete out death sentences evenhandedly.

The record since then shows the court was right the first time. When a victim's skin color is key in deciding who is put to death, the system not only violates constitutional protections but also is corrupt.

A better alternative to the death penalty is life imprisonment without parole. It protects society from those who commit heinous crimes without perpetuating a deadly system of unequal justice based on race.

Exercises

1. Outline the argument in this essay, specifying the premises and conclusion. Then write the outline of an argument that contradicts the essay's argument.

2. Write a two-page essay in which you defend a claim that contradicts the conclusion in Essay 1. For the purposes of this exercise, you may cite imaginary, but reasonable, evidence.

3. Write a three-page essay in which you assess the merits of Essay 1's argument, examining the truth of its premises and whether the conclusion follows from those premises. Take into account any possible objections to your view.

Essay 2
Marine Parks

Bill Daly

The issue of whether we should allow marine parks to stay open has been widely debated in our community recently. It is an important issue because it concerns fundamental moral and economic questions about the way we use our native wildlife. A variety of different arguments have been put forward about this issue. This essay will consider arguments for having marine parks and point to some of the problems with these views. It will then put forward reasons for the introduction of laws which prohibit these unnecessary and cruel institutions.

It has been argued that dolphin parks provide the only opportunity for much of the public to see marine mammals (Smith, 1992). Most Australians, so this argument goes, live in cities and never get to see these animals. It is claimed that marine parks allow the average Australian to appreciate our marine wildlife. However, as Smith states, dolphins, whales and seals can be viewed in the wild at a number of places on the Australian coast. In fact, there are more places where they can be seen in the wild than places where they can be seen in captivity. Moreover, most Australians would have to travel less to get to these locations than they would to get to the marine parks on the Gold Coast. In addition, places where there are wild marine mammals do not charge an exorbitant entry fee—they are free.

Dr. Alison Lane, the director of the Cairns Marine Science Institute, contends that we need marine parks for scientific research (*The Age*, 19.2.93). She argues that much of our knowledge of marine mammals comes from studies which were undertaken at marine parks. The knowledge which is obtained at marine parks, so this argument goes, can be useful for planning for the conservation of marine mammal species. However, as Jones (1991) explains, park research is only useful for understanding captive animals and is not useful for learning about animals in the wild. Dolphin and whale biology changes in marine park conditions. Their diets are different, they have significantly lower life spans and they are more prone to disease. In addition, marine mammals in dolphin parks are trained and this means that their patterns of social behaviour are changed. Therefore research undertaken at marine parks is generally not reliable.

It is the contention of the Marine Park Owners Association that marine parks attract a lot of foreign tourists (*The Sun-Herald*, 12.4.93). This position goes on to assert that these tourists spend a lot of money, increasing our foreign exchange earnings and assisting our national balance of payments. However, foreign tourists would still come to Australia if the parks were closed down. Indeed, surveys of overseas tourists show that they come here for a variety of other reasons and not to visit places like Sea World (*The Age, Good Weekend*, 16.8.93). Tourists come here to see our native wildlife in its natural environment and not to see it in cages and cement pools. They can see animals in those conditions in their own countries. Furthermore, we should be promoting our beautiful natural environment to tourists and not the ugly concrete marine park venues.

Dolphin parks are unnecessary and cruel. The dolphins and whales in these parks are kept in very small, cramped ponds, whereas in the wild they are used to roaming long distances across the seas. Furthermore, the concrete walls of the pools interfere with the animals' sonar systems of communication. In addition, keeping them in pools is a terrible restriction of the freedom of fellow creatures who may have very high levels of intelligence and a sophisticated language ability. Moreover, there are many documented cases of marine mammals helping humans who are in danger at sea or helping fisherman with their work.

In conclusion, these parks should be closed, or at the very least, no new animals should be captured for marine parks in the future. Our society is no longer prepared to tolerate unnecessary cruelty to animals for science and entertainment. If we continue with our past crimes against these creatures we will be remembered as cruel and inhuman by the generations of the future.

Bibliography

The Age, 19.2.93.

The Age, Good Weekend, 16.8.93.

Jones, G. (1991). "The Myths About Animal Research in Marine Parks." In *Scientific Australian*, Vol. 12, No. 3.

Smith, H. (1992). "Marine Parks: Good for Business, Good for Australia." In Leisure

Business Review, Vol. 24, No. 4.

The Sun-Herald, 12.4.93.

Exercises

1. Study the argument presented in this essay. Identify the conclusion and the premises and objections considered. Then write a two-page rebuttal to the essay. That is, defend the claim that marine mammals should continue to be kept in marine parks. Cite real evidence to support your argument.

2. Write an alternative opening for Essay 2. If you want, you may invent quotes or stories.

3. Write a three-page essay in which you assess the merits of Essay 2's argument, examining the truth of its premises and whether the conclusion follows from those premises.

Essay 3
A Feminist Defense of Pornography

Wendy McElroy

"Pornography benefits women, both personally and politically." This sentence opens my book *XXX: A Woman's Right to Pornography,* and it constitutes a more extreme defense of pornography than most feminists are comfortable with. I arrived at this position after years of interviewing hundreds of sex workers.

Feminist Positions

Feminist positions on pornography currently break down into three rough categories. The most common one—at least, in academia—is that pornography is an expression of male culture through which women are commodified and exploited. A second view, the liberal position, combines a respect for free speech with the principle "a woman's body, a woman's right" and thus produces a defense of pornography along the lines of, "I don't approve of it, but everyone has the right to consume or produce words and images." A third view—a true defense of pornography—arises from feminists who have been labeled "pro-sex" and who argue that porn has benefits for women.

Little dialogue occurs between the three positions. Anti-pornography feminists treat women who disagree as either brainwashed dupes of patriarchy or as apologists for pornographers. In the anthology *Sexual Liberals and the Attack on Feminism* (1990), editor Dorchen Leidholdt claims that feminists who believe women make their own choices about pornography are spreading "a felicitous lie" (p. 131). In the same work, Sheila Jeffreys argues that "pro-sex" feminists are "eroticizing dominance and subordination." Wendy Stock accuses free speech feminists of identifying with their oppressors "much like . . . concentration camp prisoners with their jailors" (p. 150). Andrea Dworkin accuses them of running a "sex protection racket" (p. 136) and maintains that no one who defends pornography can be a feminist.

The liberal feminists who are personally uncomfortable with pornography tend to be intimidated into silence. Those who continue to speak out, like American Civil Liberties Union President Nadine Strossen (*Defending Pornography*) are ignored. For example, Catharine MacKinnon has repeatedly refused to share a stage with Strossen or any woman who defends porn. "Pro-sex" feminists—many of whom are current or former sex-workers—often respond with anger, rather than arguments.

Peeling back the emotions, what are the substantive questions raised by each feminist perspective?

Anti-porn feminism

Page Mellish of Feminists Fighting Pornography has declared, "There's no feminist issue that isn't rooted in the porn problem." In her book *Only Words*, MacKinnon denies that pornography consists of words and images, both of which would be protected by the First Amendment. She considers pornography—in and of itself—to be an act of sexual violence. Why is pornography viewed as both the core issue of modern feminism and an inherent act of violence? The answer lies in radical feminist ideology, which Christina Hoff Sommers calls "gender feminism."

Gender feminism looks at history and sees an uninterrupted oppression of women by men that spans cultural barriers. To them, the only feasible explanation is that men and women are separate and antagonistic classes whose interests necessarily conflict. Male interests are expressed through and maintained by a capitalistic structure known as "patriarchy."

The root of the antagonism is so deep that it lies in male biology itself. For example, in the watershed book *Against Our Will*, Susan Brownmiller traces the inevitability of rape back to Neanderthal times when men began to use their penises as weapons. Brownmiller writes: "From prehistoric times to the present, I believe, rape has played a critical function. It is nothing more or less than a conscious process of intimidation by which all men keep all women in a state of fear." How Brownmiller acquired this knowledge of prehistoric sex is not known.

Another tenet of gender oppression is that sex is a social construct. Radical feminists reject what they call "sexual essentialism"—the notion that sex is a natural force based on biology that inclines women toward natural tendencies, such as motherhood. Even deeply felt sexual preferences, such as heterosexuality, are not biological. They spring from ideology.

Men construct women's sexuality through the words and images of society, which the French philosopher Foucault called the "texts" of society. After such construction, men commercialize women's sexuality and market it back in the form of pornography. In other words, through porn man defines woman sexually—a definition that determines every aspect of her role in society. To end the oppression, patriarchy and its texts must be destroyed.

Liberal Feminism

Liberal feminism is a continuation of 1960s feminism that called for equality with men, who were not inherent oppressors so much as recalcitrant partners to be enlightened. Equality did not mean destroying the current system, but reforming it through such measures as affirmative action. The liberal principle "a woman's body, a woman's right" underlay arguments ranging from abortion rights to lifestyle freedoms like lesbianism. The stress was upon the act of choosing, rather than upon the content of any choice.

Liberal feminists share the general liberal bias toward free speech, but they are in flux on pornography. Some liberal organizations like Feminists for Free Expression (FFE) have consistently opposed censorship in any form. Some liberal feminists like Sallie Tisdale (*Talk Dirty to Me*) have staunchly defended sexual freedom. But many liberal feminists commonly reason as follows: "As a woman I am appalled by *Playboy* . . . but as a writer I understand the need for free expression."

Such arguments are not pro-pornography. They are anti-censorship ones based on several grounds, including: great works of art and literature would be banned; the First Amendment would be breached; political expression would be suppressed; and a creative culture requires freedom of speech.

Other liberal feminists, who have accepted many of the ideological assumptions of the anti-porn position, seem willing to sacrifice free speech for the greater good of protecting women. For example, they also condemn the free market for commercializing women as "body parts," which demeans women. In "A Capital Idea," an essay defending pornography, which sometimes seems to be an attack, Lisa Steel comments:

Sexist representation of women . . . is all part of the same system that, in the service of profits, reduces society to "consumer groups." And marketing is every bit as conservative as the military . . . we pay dearly for the "rights" of a few to make profits from the rest of us.

Such muddled and ambivalent "defenses" often offend the sex workers they are intended to protect.

Pro-sex feminism

Over the past decade, a growing number of feminists—labeled "pro sex"—have defended a woman's choice to participate in and to consume pornography. Some of these women, such as Nina Hartley, are current or ex-sex-workers who know firsthand that posing for pornography is an uncoerced choice that can be enriching. Pro-sex feminists retain a consistent interpretation of the principle "a woman's body, a woman's right" and insist that every peaceful choice a woman makes with her own body must be accorded full legal protection, if not respect.

Pro-sex arguments sometimes seem to overlap with liberal feminist ones. For example, both express concern over who will act as censor because subjective words, such as "degrading," will be interpreted to mean whatever the censor wishes.

The statute that banned Margaret Sanger because she used the words *syphilis* and *gonorrhea* is no different, in principle, than the one that interprets obscenity today. There will be no protection even for the classics of feminism, such as *Our Bodies, Ourselves*, which provided a generation of women with the first explicit view of their own biology. Inevitably, censorship will be used against the least popular views, against the weakest members of society . . . including feminists and lesbians. When the Canadian Supreme Court decided in 1992 to protect women by restricting the importation of pornography, one of the first victims was the lesbian/gay Glad Day Bookstore, which had been on a police hit list. Among the books seized by Canadian customs were two books by Andrea Dworkin, *Pornography: Men Possessing Women* and *Women Hating*. Such an event should not have surprised Dworkin who declared in *Take Back the Night*, "There is not a feminist alive who could possibly look to the male legal system for real protection from the systematized sadism of men" (p. 257).

On the dangers of censoring pornography, pro-sex and liberal feminists often agree. On the possible benefits of pornography to women, they part company.

Dissecting Anti-Porn

Do the specific accusations hurled at pornography stand up under examination?

Pornography Is degrading to women.

Degrading is a subjective term. I find commercials in which women become orgasmic over soapsuds to be tremendously degrading. The bottom line is that every woman has the right to define what is degrading and liberating for herself.

The assumed degradation is often linked to the "objectification" of women: that is, porn converts them into sexual objects. What does this mean? If taken literally, it means nothing because objects don't have sexuality; only beings do. But to say that porn portrays women as "sexual beings" makes for poor rhetoric. Usually, the term *sex objects* means showing women as body parts, reducing them to physical objects. What is wrong with this? Women are as much their bodies as they are their minds or souls. No one gets upset if you present women as "brains" or as spiritual beings. If I concentrated on a woman's sense of humor to the exclusion of her other characteristics, is this degrading? Why is it degrading to focus on her sexuality?

Pornography leads to violence against women.

A cause-and-effect relationship is drawn between men viewing pornography and men attacking women, especially in the form of rape. But studies and experts disagree as to whether any relationship exists between pornography and violence, between images and behavior. Even the pro-censorship Meese Commission Report admitted that the data connecting pornography to violence was unreliable.

Other studies, such as the one prepared by feminist Thelma McCormick in 1983 for the Metropolitan Toronto Task Force on Violence Against Women, find no pattern to connect porn and sex crimes. Incredibly, the Task Force suppressed the study and reassigned the project to a pro-censorship male, who returned the "correct" results. His study was published.

What of real-world feedback? In Japan, where pornography depicting graphic and brutal violence is widely available, rape is much lower per capita than in the United States, where violence in porn is severely restricted.

Pornography is violence because women are coerced into pornography

Not one of the dozens of women depicted in pornographic materials with whom I spoke reported being coerced. Not one knew of a woman who had been. Nevertheless, I do not dismiss reports of violence: every industry has its abuses. And anyone who uses force or threats to make a woman perform should be charged with kidnapping, assault, and/or rape. Any such pictures or films should be confiscated and burned because no one has the right to benefit from the proceeds of a crime.

Pornography is violence because women who pose for porn are so traumatized by patriarchy they cannot give real consent.

Although women in pornography appear to be willing, anti-porn feminists know that no psychologically healthy woman would agree to the degradation of pornography. Therefore, if agreement seems to be present, it is because the women have "fallen in love with their own oppression" and must be rescued from themselves. A common characteristic of the porn actresses I have interviewed is a love of exhibitionism. Yet if such a woman declares her enjoyment in flaunting her body, anti-porn feminists claim she is not merely a unique human being who reacts from a different background or personality. She is psychologically damaged and no longer responsible for her actions. In essence, this is a denial of a woman's right to choose anything outside the narrow corridor of choices offered by political/sexual correctness. The right to choose hinges on the right to make a "wrong" choice, just as freedom of religion entails the right to be an atheist. After all, no one will prevent a woman from doing what she thinks she should do.

A Pro-Sex Defense

As a "pro-sex" feminist, I contend: Pornography benefits women, both personally and politically. It provides sexual information on at least three levels:

1. It gives a panoramic view of the world's sexual possibilities. This is true even of basic sexual information such as masturbation. It is not uncommon for women to reach adulthood without knowing how to give themselves pleasure.

2. It allows women to "safely" experience sexual alternatives and satisfy a healthy sexual curiosity. The world is a dangerous place. By contrast, pornography can be a source of solitary enlightenment.

3. It offers the emotional information that comes only from experiencing something either directly or vicariously. It provides us with a sense how it would "feel" to do something.

Pornography allows women to enjoy scenes and situations that would be anathema to them in real life. Take, for example, one of the most common fantasies reported by women—the fantasy of "being taken." The first thing to understand is that a rape fantasy does not represent a desire for the real thing. Why would a healthy woman daydream about being raped? Perhaps by losing control, she also sheds all sense of responsibility for and guilt over sex. Perhaps it is the exact opposite of the polite, gentle sex she has now. Perhaps it is flattering to imagine a particular man being so overwhelmed by her that he must have her. Perhaps she is curious. Perhaps she has some masochistic feelings that are vented through the fantasy. Is it better to bottle them up?

Pornography breaks cultural and political stereotypes, so that each woman can interpret sex for herself. Anti-feminists tell women to be ashamed of their appetites and urges. Pornography tells them to accept and enjoy them.

Pornography can be good therapy. Pornography provides a sexual outlet for those who—for whatever reason—have no sexual partner. Perhaps they are away from home, recently widowed, isolated because of infirmity. Perhaps they simply choose to be alone. Couples also use pornography to enhance their relationships. Sometimes they do so on their own, watching videos and exploring their reactions together. Sometimes, the couples go to a sex therapist who advises them to use pornography as a way of opening up communication on sex.

By sharing pornography, the couples are able to experience variety in their sex lives without having to commit adultery.

Pornography benefits women politically in many ways. Historically, pornography and feminism have been fellow travelers and natural allies. Although it is not possible to draw a cause-and-effect relationship between the rise of pornography and that of feminism, they both demand the same social conditions—namely, sexual freedom.

Pornography is free speech applied to the sexual realm. Freedom of speech is the ally of those who seek change: it is the enemy of those who seek to maintain control. Pornography, along with all other forms of sexual heresy, such as homosexuality, should have the same legal protection as political heresy. This protection is especially important to women, whose sexuality has been controlled by censorship through the centuries.

Viewing pornography may well have a cathartic effect on men who have violent urges toward women. If this is true, restricting pornography removes a protective barrier between women and abuse.

Legitimizing pornography would protect female sex-workers, who are stigmatized by our society. Anti-pornography feminists are actually undermining the safety of sex workers when they treat them as "indoctrinated women." Dr. Leonore Tiefer, a professor of psychology, observed in her essay "On Censorship and Women": "These women have appealed to feminists for support, not rejection. . . . Sex industry workers, like all women, are striving for economic survival and a decent life, and if feminism means anything it means sisterhood and solidarity with these women."

The Purpose of Law

The porn debate is underscored by two fundamentally antagonistic views of the purpose of law in society.

The first view, to which pro-sex feminists subscribe, is that law should protect choice. "A woman's body, a woman's right" applies to every peaceful activity a woman chooses to engage in. The law should come into play only when a woman initiates force or has force initiated against her. The second view, to which both conservatives and anti-porn feminists subscribe, is that law should protect virtue. It should come into play whenever there has been a breach of public morality, or a breach of "women's class interests."

This is old whine in new battles. The issue at stake in the pornography debate is nothing less than the age-old conflict between individual freedom and social control.

Exercises

1. Create an outline for this essay. Specify the thesis statement, each premise, support for the premises, any objections considered, and the conclusion.

2. Write a summary of Essay 3 in 75 to 100 words, specifying the premises and conclusion.

3. Write a three-page assessment of the argument, evaluating the truth of the premises and conclusion and the logic of the argument as a whole. Address possible objections to your view.

Essay 4
A Defense of Homosexuality

John Corvino

Tommy and Jim are a homosexual couple I know. Tommy is an accountant; Jim is a botany professor. They are in their forties and have been together fourteen years, the last five of which they've lived in a Victorian house that they've lovingly restored. Although their relationship has had its challenges, each has made sacrifices for the sake of the other's happiness and the relationship's long-term success.

I assume that Tommy and Jim have sex with each other (although I've never bothered to ask). Furthermore, I contend that they probably *should* have sex with each other. For one thing, sex is pleasurable. But it is also much more than that: a sexual relationship can unite two people in a way that virtually nothing else can. It can be an avenue of growth, of communication, and of lasting interpersonal fulfillment. These are reasons why most heterosexual couples have sex even if they don't want children, don't want children yet, or don't want additional children. And if these reasons are good enough for most heterosexual couples, then they should be good enough for Tommy and Jim.

Of course, having a reason to do something does not preclude there being an even better reason for not doing it. Tommy might have a good reason for drinking orange juice (it's tasty and nutritious) but an even better reason for not doing so (he's allergic). The point is that one would need a pretty good reason for denying a sexual relationship to Tommy and Jim, given the intense benefits widely associated with such relationships. The question I shall consider in this paper is thus quite simple Why shouldn't Tommy and Jim have sex?[1]

Homosexual Sex Is "Unnatural"

Many contend that homosexual sex is "unnatural." But what does that mean? Many things that people value—clothing, houses, medicine, and government, for example—are unnatural in some sense. On the other hand, many things that people detest—disease, suffering, and death, for example—are "natural" in the sense that they occur "in nature." If the unnaturalness charge is to be more than empty rhetorical flourish, those who levy it must specify what they mean. Borrowing from Burton Leiser, I will examine several possible meanings of "unnatural."[2]

What is unusual or abnormal is unnatural.

One meaning of "unnatural" refers to that which deviates from the norm, that is, from what most people do. Obviously, most people, engage in heterosexual relationships. But does it follow that it is wrong to engage in homosexual relationships? Relatively few people read Sanskrit, pilot ships, play the mandolin, breed goats, or write with both hands, yet none of these activities is immoral simply because it is unusual. As the Ramsey Colloquium, a group of Jewish and Christian scholars who oppose homosexuality, writes, "The statistical frequency of an act does not determine its moral status."[3] So while homosexuality might be unnatural in the sense of being unusual, that fact is morally irrelevant.

What is not practiced by other animals is unnatural.

Some people argue, "Even animals know better than to behave homosexually; homosexuality must be wrong." This argument is doubly flawed. First, it rests on a false premise. Numerous studies—including Anne Perkins's study of "gay" sheep and George and Molly Hunt's study of "lesbian" sea gulls—have shown that some animals do form homosexual pair-bonds.[4] Second, even if animals did not behave homosexually, that fact would not prove that homosexuality is immoral. After all, animals don't cook their food, brush their teeth, participate in religious worship, or attend college; human beings do all these without moral censure. Indeed, the idea that animals could provide us with our standards—especially our sexual standards—is simply amusing.

What does not proceed from innate desires is unnatural.

Recent studies suggesting a biological basis for homosexuality have resulted in two popular positions. One side proposes that homosexual people are "born that way" and that it is therefore natural (and thus good) for them to form homosexual relationships. The other side maintains that homosexuality is a lifestyle choice, which is therefore unnatural (and thus wrong). Both sides assume a connection between the origin of homosexual orientation, on the one hand, and the moral value of homosexual activity, on the other. And insofar as they share that assumption, both sides are wrong.

Consider first the pro-homosexual side: "They are born that way; therefore it's natural and good." This inference assumes that all innate desires are good ones (i.e., that they should be acted upon). But that assumption is clearly false. Research suggests that some people are born with a predisposition toward violence, but such people have no more right to strangle their neighbors than anyone else. So while people like Tommy and Jim may be born with homosexual tendencies, it doesn't follow that they *ought* to act on them. Nor does it follow that they ought not to act on them, even if the tendencies are not innate. I probably do not have any innate tendency to write with my left hand (since I, like everyone else in my family, have always been right-handed), but it doesn't follow that it would be immoral for me to do so. So simply asserting that homosexuality is a lifestyle choice will not show that it is an immoral lifestyle choice.

Do people "choose" to be homosexual? People certainly don't seem to choose their sexual *feelings*, at least not in any direct or obvious way. (Do you? Think about it.) Rather, they find certain people attractive and certain activities arousing, whether they "decide" to or not. Indeed, most people at some point in their lives wish that they could control their feelings more—for example, in situations of unrequited love—and find it frustrating that they cannot. What they can control to a considerable degree is how and when they act upon those feelings. In that sense, both homosexuality and heterosexuality involve lifestyle choices. But in either case, determining the origin of the feelings will not determine whether it is moral to act on them.

What violates an organ's principal purpose is unnatural.

Perhaps when people claim that homosexual sex is unnatural they mean that it cannot result in procreation. The idea behind the argument is that human organs have various natural purposes: eyes are for seeing, ears are for hearing, genitals are for procreating. According to this argument, it is immoral to use an organ in a way that violates its particular purpose.

Many of our organs, however, have multiple purposes. Tommy can use his mouth for talking, eating, breathing, licking stamps, chewing gum, kissing women, or kissing Jim; and it seems rather arbitrary to claim that all but the last use are "natural."[5] (And if we say that some of the other uses are "unnatural, but not immoral," we have failed to specify a morally relevant sense of the term "natural.")

Just because people can and do use their sexual organs to procreate, it does not follow that they should not use them for other purposes. Sexual organs seem very well suited for expressing love, for giving and receiving pleasure, and for celebrating, replenishing, and enhancing a relationship—even when procreation is not a factor. Unless opponents of homosexuality are prepared to condemn heterosexual couples who use contraception or individuals who masturbate, they must abandon this version of the unnaturalness argument. Indeed, even the Roman Catholic Church, which forbids contraception and masturbation, approves of sex for sterile couples and of sex during pregnancy, neither of which can lead to procreation. The Church concedes here that intimacy and pleasure are morally legitimate purposes for sex, even in cases where procreation is impossible. But since homosexual sex can achieve these purposes as well, it is inconsistent for the Church to condemn it on the grounds that it is not procreative.

One might object that sterile heterosexual couples do not *intentionally* turn away from pro-creation, whereas homosexual couples do. But this distinction doesn't hold. It is no more possible for Tommy to procreate with a woman whose uterus has been removed than it is for him to procreate with Jim.[6] By having sex with either one, he is intentionally engaging in a nonprocreative sexual act.

Yet one might press the objection further and insist that Tommy and the woman *could* produce children if the woman were fertile: whereas homosexual relationships are essentially infertile, heterosexual relationships are only incidentally so. But what does that prove? Granted, it might require less of a miracle for a woman without a uterus to become pregnant than for Jim to become pregnant, but it would require a miracle nonetheless. Thus it seems that the real difference here is not that one couple is fertile and the other not, nor that one couple "could" be fertile (with the help of a miracle) and the other not, but rather that one couple is male-female and the other male-male. In other words, sex between Tommy and Jim is wrong because it's male-male—i.e., because it's homosexual. But that, of course, is no argument at all.[7]

What is disgusting or offensive is unnatural.

It often seems that when people call homosexuality "unnatural" they really just mean it's disgusting. But plenty of morally neutral activities—handling snakes, eating snails, performing autopsies, cleaning toilets, and so on—disgust people. Indeed, for centuries, most people found interracial relationships disgusting, yet that feeling—which has by no means disappeared—hardly proves that such relationships are wrong. In sum, the charge that homosexuality is unnatural, at least in its most common forms, is longer on rhetorical flourish than on philosophical cogency. At best it expresses an aesthetic judgment, not a moral judgment.

Homosexual Sex Is Harmful

One might instead argue that homosexuality is harmful. The Ramsey Colloquium, for instance, argues that homosexuality leads to the breakdown of the family and, ultimately, of human society, and it points to the "alarming rates of sexual promiscuity, depression, and suicide and the ominous presence of AIDS within the homosexual subculture."[8] Thomas Schmidt marshals copious statistics to show that homosexual activity undermines physical and psychological health.[9] Such charges, if correct, would seem to provide strong evidence against homosexuality. But are the charges correct? And do they prove what they purport to prove?

One obvious (and obviously problematic) way to answer the first question is to ask people like Tommy and Jim. It would appear that no one is in a better position to judge the homosexual lifestyle than those who know it firsthand. Yet it is unlikely that critics would trust their testimony. Indeed, the more homosexual people try to explain their lives, the more critics accuse them of deceitfully promoting an agenda. (It's like trying to prove that you're not crazy. The more you object, the more people think, "That's exactly what a crazy person would say.")

One might instead turn to statistics. An obvious problem with this tack is that both sides of the debate bring forth extensive statistics and "expert" testimony, leaving the average observer confused. There is a more subtle problem as well. Because of widespread antigay sentiment, many homosexual people won't acknowledge their romantic feelings to themselves, much less to researchers.[10] I have known a number of gay men who did not "come out" until their forties and fifties, and no amount of professional competence on the part of interviewers would have been likely to open their closets sooner. Such problems compound the usual difficulties of finding representative population samples for statistical study.

Yet even if the statistical claims of gay rights opponents were true, they would not prove what they purport to prove, for several reasons. First, as any good statistician realizes, correlation does not equal cause. Even if homosexual people were more likely to commit suicide, be promiscuous, or contract AIDS than the general population, it would not follow that their homosexuality causes them to do these things. An alternative—and very plausible—explanation is that these phenomena, like the disproportionately high crime rates among African Americans, are at least partly a function of society's treatment of the group in question. Suppose you were told from a very early age that the romantic feelings that you experienced were sick, unnatural, and disgusting. Suppose further that expressing these feelings put you at risk of social ostracism or, worse yet, physical violence. Is it not plausible that you would, for instance, be more inclined to depression than you would be without such obstacles? And that such depression could, in its extreme forms, lead to suicide or other self-destructive behaviors? (It is indeed remarkable that couples like Tommy and Jim continue to flourish in the face of such obstacles.)

A similar explanation can be given for the alleged promiscuity of homosexuals.[11] The denial of legal marriage, the pressure to remain in the closet, and the overt hostility toward homosexual relationships are all more conducive to transient, clandestine encounters than they are to long-term unions. As a result, that which is challenging enough for heterosexual couples—settling down and building a life together—becomes far more challenging for homosexual couples.

Indeed, there is an interesting tension in the critics' position here. Opponents of homosexuality commonly claim that "marriage and the family . . . are fragile institutions in need of careful and continuing support."[12] And they point to the increasing prevalence of divorce and premarital sex among heterosexuals as evidence that such support is declining. Yet they refuse to concede that the complete absence of similar support for homosexual relationships might explain many of the alleged problems of homosexuals. The critics can't have it both ways: if heterosexual marriages are in trouble despite the various social, economic, and legal incentives for keeping them together, society should be little surprised that homosexual relationships—which not only lack such supports, but face overt hostility—are difficult to maintain.

One might object that if social ostracism were the main cause of homosexual people's problems, then homosexual people in more "tolerant" cities like New York and San Francisco should exhibit fewer such problems than their smalltown counterparts; yet statistics do not seem to bear this out. This objection underestimates the extent of antigay sentiment in our society. By the time many gay and lesbian people move to urban centers, they have already been exposed to (and may have internalized) considerable hostility toward homosexuality. Moreover, the visibility of homosexuality in urban centers makes gay and lesbian people there more vulnerable to attack (and thus more likely to exhibit certain difficulties). Finally, note that urbanites *in general* (not just homosexual urbanites) tend to exhibit higher rates of promiscuity, depression, and sexually transmitted disease than the rest of the population.

But what about AIDS? Opponents of homosexuality sometimes claim that even if homosexual sex is not, strictly speaking, immoral, it is still a bad idea, since it puts people at risk for AIDS and other sexually transmitted diseases. But that claim is misleading: it is infinitely more risky for Tommy to have sex with a woman who is HIV-positive than with Jim, who is HIV-negative. Obviously, it's not homosexuality that's harmful, it's the virus; and the virus may be carried by both heterosexual and homosexual people.

Now it may be true (in the United States, at least) that homosexual males are statistically more likely to carry the virus than heterosexual females and thus that homosexual sex is *statistically* more risky than heterosexual sex (in cases where the partner's HIV status is unknown). But opponents of homosexuality need something stronger than this statistical claim. For if it is wrong for men to have sex with men because their doing so puts them at a higher AIDS risk than heterosexual sex, then it is also wrong for women to have sex with men because their doing so puts them at a higher AIDS risk than homosexual sex (lesbians as a group have the lowest incidence of AIDS). Purely from the standpoint of AIDS risk, women ought to prefer lesbian sex.

If this response seems silly, it is because there is obviously more to choosing a romantic or sexual partner than determining AIDS risk. And a major part of the decision, one that opponents of homosexuality consistently overlook, is considering whether one can have a mutually fulfilling relationship with the partner. For many people like Tommy and Jim, such fulfillment—which most heterosexuals recognize to be an important component of human flourishing—is only possible with members of the same sex.

Of course, the foregoing argument hinges on the claim that homosexual sex can only cause harm indirectly. Some would object that there are certain activities—anal sex, for instance—that for anatomical reasons are intrinsically harmful. But an argument against anal intercourse is by no means tantamount to an argument against homosexuality: neither all nor only homosexuals engage in anal sex. There are plenty of other things for both gay men and lesbians to do in bed. Indeed, for women, it appears that the most common forms of homosexual activity may be less risky than penile-vaginal intercourse, since the latter has been linked to cervical cancer.[13]

In sum, there is nothing *inherently* risky about sex between persons of the same gender. It is only risky under certain conditions: for instance, if they exchange diseased bodily fluids or if they engage in certain "rough" forms of sex that could cause tearing of delicate tissue. Heterosexual sex is equally risky under such conditions. Thus, even if statistical claims like those of Schmidt and the Ramsey Colloquium were true, they would not prove that homosexuality is immoral. At best, they would prove that homosexual people—like everyone else—ought to take great care when deciding to become sexually active.

Of course, there's more to a flourishing life than avoiding harm. One might argue that even if Tommy and Jim are not harming each other by their relationship, they are still failing to achieve the higher level of fulfillment possible in a heterosexual relationship, which is rooted in the complementarity of male and female. But this argument just ignores the facts: Tommy and Jim are homosexual *precisely because* they find relationships with men (and, in particular, with each other) more fulfilling than relationships with women. Even evangelicals (who have long advocated "faith healing" for homosexuals) are beginning to acknowledge that the choice for most homosexual people is not between homosexual relationships and heterosexual relationships, but rather between homosexual relationships and celibacy.[14] What the critics need to show, therefore, is that no matter how loving, committed, mutual, generous, and fulfilling the relationship may be, Tommy and Jim would flourish more if they were celibate. Given the evidence of their lives (and of others like them), this is a formidable task indeed.

Thus far I have focused on the allegation that homosexuality harms those who engage in it. But what about the allegation that homosexuality harms other, non-consenting parties? Here I will briefly consider two claims: that homosexuality threatens children and that it threatens society.

Those who argue that homosexuality threatens children may mean one of two things. First, they may mean that homosexual people are child molesters. Statistically, the vast majority of reported cases of child sexual abuse involve young girls and their fathers, stepfathers, or other familiar (and presumably heterosexual) adult males.[15] But opponents of homosexuality argue that when one adjusts for relative percentage in the population, homosexual males appear more likely than heterosexual males to be child molesters. As I argued above, the problems with obtaining reliable statistics on homosexuality render such calculations difficult. Fortunately, they are also unnecessary.

Child abuse is a terrible thing. But when a heterosexual male molests a child (or rapes a woman or commits assault), the act does not reflect upon all heterosexuals. Similarly, when a homosexual male molests a child, there is no reason why that act should reflect upon all homosexuals. Sex with adults of the same sex is one thing; sex with *children* of the same sex is quite another. Conflating the two not only slanders innocent people, it also misdirects resources intended to protect children. Furthermore, many men convicted of molesting young boys are sexually attracted to adult women and report no attraction to adult men.[16] To call such men "homosexual," or even "bisexual," is probably to stretch such terms too far[17]

Alternatively, those who charge that homosexuality threatens children might mean that the increasing visibility of homosexual relationships makes children more likely to become homosexual. The argument for this view is patently circular. One cannot prove that doing X is bad by arguing that it causes other people to do X, which is bad. One must first establish independently that X is bad. That said, there is not a shred of evidence to demonstrate that exposure to homosexuality leads children to become homosexual.

But doesn't homosexuality threaten society? A Roman Catholic priest once put the argument to me as follows; "Of course homosexuality is bad for society. If everyone were homosexual, there would be no society." Perhaps it is true that if everyone were homosexual, there would be no society. But if everyone were a celibate priest, society would collapse just as surely, and my friend the priest didn't seem to think he was doing anything wrong simply by failing to procreate. Jeremy Bentham made the point somewhat more acerbically roughly 200 years ago: "If then merely out of regard to population it were right that [homosexuals] should be burnt alive, monks ought to be roasted alive by a slow fire."[18]

From the fact that the continuation of society requires procreation, it does not follow that *everyone* must procreate. Moreover, even if such an obligation existed, it would not preclude homosexuality. At best, it would preclude *exclusive* homosexuality: homosexual people who occasionally have heterosexual sex can procreate just fine. And given artificial insemination, even those who are exclusively homosexual can procreate. In short, the priest's claim—if everyone were homosexual, there would be no society—is false; and even if it were true, it would not establish that homosexuality is immoral.

The Ramsey Colloquium commits a similar fallacy.[19] Noting (correctly) that heterosexual marriage promotes the continuation of human life, it then infers that homosexuality is immoral because it fails to accomplish the same.[20] But from the fact that procreation is good, it does not follow that childlessness is bad—a point that the members of the colloquium, several of whom are Roman Catholic priests, should readily concede.

I have argued that Tommy and Jim's sexual relationship harms neither them nor society. On the contrary, it benefits both. It benefits them because it makes them happier—not merely in a short-term, hedonistic sense, but in a long-term, "big picture" sort of way. And, in turn, it benefits society, since it makes Tommy and Jim more stable, more productive, and more generous than they would otherwise be. In short, their relationship—including its sexual component—provides the same kinds of benefits that infertile heterosexual relationships provide (and perhaps other benefits as well). Nor should we fear that accepting their relationship and others like it will cause people to flee in droves from the institution of heterosexual marriage. After all, as Thomas Williams points out, the usual response to a gay person is not "How come *he* gets to be gay and I don't?"[21]

Homosexuality Violates Biblical Teaching

At this point in the discussion, many people turn to religion. "If the secular arguments fail to prove that homosexuality is wrong," they say, "so much the worse for secular ethics. This failure only proves that we need God for morality." Since people often justify their moral beliefs by appeal to religion, I will briefly consider the biblical position.

At first glance, the Bible's condemnation of homosexual activity seems unequivocal. Consider, for example, the following two passages, one from the "Old" Testament and one from the "New":[22]

> *You shall not lie with a male as with a woman; it is an abomination. (Lev. 18:22)*

> *For this reason God gave them up to degrading passions. Their women exchanged natural intercourse for unnatural, and in the same way also the men, giving up natural intercourse with women, were consumed with passion for one another. Men committed shameless acts with men and received in their own persons the due penalty for their error. (Rom. 1:26–27)*

Note, however, that these passages are surrounded by other passages that relatively few people consider binding. For example, Leviticus also declares,

> *The pig . . . is unclean for you. Of their flesh you shall not eat, and their carcasses you shall not touch; they are unclean for you. (11:7–8)*

Taken literally, this passage not only prohibits eating pork, but also playing football, since footballs are made of pigskin. (Can you believe that the University of Notre Dame so flagrantly violates Levitical teaching?)

Similarly, St. Paul, author of the Romans passage, also writes, "Slaves, obey your earthly masters with fear and trembling, in singleness of heart, as you obey Christ" (Eph. 6:5)—morally problematic advice if there ever were any. Should we interpret this passage (as Southern plantation owners once did) as implying that it is immoral for slaves to escape? After all, God himself says in Leviticus,

[Y]ou may acquire male and female slaves . . . from among the aliens residing with you, and from their families that are with you, who have been born in your land; and they may be your property. You may keep them as a possession for your children after you, for them to inherit as property. (25:44–46)

How can people maintain the inerrancy of the Bible in light of such passages? The answer, I think, is that they learn to interpret the passages *in their historical context.*

Consider the Bible's position on usury, the lending of money for interest (for *any* interest, not just excessive interest). The Bible condemns this practice in no uncertain terms. In Exodus God says that "if you lend money to my people, to the poor among you, you shall not exact interest from them" (22:25). Psalm 15 says that those who lend at interest may not abide in the Lord's tent or dwell on his holy hill (1–5). Ezekiel calls usury "abominable"; compares it to adultery, robbery, idolatry, and bribery; and states that anyone who "takes advanced or accrued interest . . . shall surely die; his blood shall be upon himself" (18:13).[23]

Should believers therefore close their savings accounts? Not necessarily. According to orthodox Christian teaching, the biblical prohibition against usury no longer applies. The reason is that economic conditions have changed substantially since biblical times, such that usury no longer has the same negative consequences it had when the prohibitions were issued. Thus, the practice that was condemned by the Bible differs from contemporary interest banking in morally relevant ways.[24]

Yet are we not in a similar position regarding homosexuality? Virtually all scholars agree that homosexual relations during biblical times were vastly different from relationships like Tommy and Jim's. Often such relations were integral to pagan practices. In Greek society, they typically involved older men and younger boys. If those are the kinds of features that the biblical authors had in mind when they issued their condemnations, and such features are no longer typical, then the biblical condemnations no longer apply. As with usury, substantial changes in cultural context have altered the meaning and consequences—and thus the moral value—of the practice in question. Put another way, using the Bible's condemnations of homosexuality against contemporary homosexuality is like using its condemnations of usury against contemporary banking.

Let me be clear about what I am *not* claiming here. First, I am not claiming that the Bible has been wrong before and therefore may be wrong this time. The Bible may indeed be wrong on some matters, but for the purpose of this argument I am assuming its infallibility. Nor am I claiming that the Bible's age renders it entirely inapplicable to today's issues. Rather, I am claiming that when we do apply it, *we must pay attention to morally relevant cultural differences between biblical times and today.* Such attention will help us distinguish between specific time-bound prohibitions (for example, laws against usury or homosexual relations) and the enduring moral values they represent (for example, generosity or respect for persons). And as the above argument shows, my claim is not very controversial. Indeed, to deny it is to commit oneself to some rather strange views on slavery, usury, women's roles, astronomy, evolution, and the like.

Here, one might also make an appeal to religious pluralism. Given the wide variety of religious beliefs (e.g., the Muslim belief that women should cover their faces, the Orthodox Jewish belief against working on Saturday, the Hindu belief that cows are sacred and should not be eaten), each of us inevitably violates the religious beliefs of others. But we normally don't view such violations as occasions for moral censure, since we distinguish between beliefs that depend on particular revelations and beliefs that can be justified independently (e.g., that stealing is wrong). Without an independent justification for condemning homosexuality, the best one can say is, "My religion says so." But in a society that cherishes religious freedom, that reason alone does not normally provide grounds for moral or legal sanctions. That people still fall back on that reason in discussions of homosexuality suggests that they may not have much of a case otherwise.

Conclusion

As a last resort, opponents of homosexuality typically change the subject: "But what about incest, polygamy, and bestiality? If we accept Tommy and Jim's sexual relationship, why shouldn't we accept those as well?" Opponents of interracial marriage used a similar slippery-slope argument in the 1960s when the Supreme Court struck down antimiscegenation laws.[25] It was a bad argument then, and it is a bad argument now.

Just because there are no good reasons to oppose interracial or homosexual relationships, it does not follow that there are no good reasons to oppose incestuous, polygamous, or bestial relationships. One might argue, for instance, that incestuous relationships threaten delicate familial bonds, or that polygamous relationships result in unhealthy jealousies (and sexism), or that bestial relationships—do I need to say it?—aren't really "relationships" at all, at least not in the sense we've been discussing.[26] Perhaps even better arguments could be offered (given much more space than I have here). The point is that there is no logical connection between homosexuality, on the one hand, and incest, polygamy, and bestiality, on the other.

Why, then, do critics continue to push this objection? Perhaps it's because accepting homosexuality requires them to give up one of their favorite arguments: "It's wrong because we've always been taught that it's wrong." This argument—call it the argument from tradition—has an obvious appeal: people reasonably favor tried-and-true ideas over unfamiliar ones, and they recognize the foolishness of trying to invent morality from scratch. But the argument from tradition is also a dangerous argument, as any honest look at history will reveal.

I conclude that Tommy and Jim's relationship, far from being a moral abomination, is exactly what it appears to be to those who know them: a morally positive influence on their lives and on others. Accepting this conclusion takes courage, since it entails that our moral traditions are fallible. But when these traditions interfere with people's happiness for no sound reason, they defeat what is arguably the very point of morality: promoting individual and communal well-being. To put the argument simply, Tommy and Jim's relationship makes them better people. And that's not just good for Tommy and Jim: that's good for everyone.

Notes

1. Although my central example in the paper is a gay male couple, much of what I say will apply mutatis mutandis to lesbians as well, since many of the same arguments are used against them. This is not to say gay male sexuality and lesbian sexuality are largely similar or that discussions of the former will cover all that needs to be said about the latter. Furthermore, the fact that I focus on a long-term, committed relationship should not be taken to imply any judgment about homosexual activity outside of such unions. If the argument of this paper is successful, then the evaluation of homosexual activity outside of committed unions should be largely (if not entirely) similar to the evaluation of *hetero*sexual activity outside of committed unions.

2. Burton M. Leiser, *Liberty, Justice, and Morals: Contemporary Value Conflicts* (New York: Macmillan, 1986), 51–57.

3. The Ramsey Colloquium, "The Homosexual Movement," *First Things* (March 1994), 15–20.

4. For an overview of some of these studies, see Simon LeVay, *Queer Science* (Boston: MIT Press, 1996), chap. 10.

5. I have borrowed some items in this list from Richard Mohr's pioneering work *Gays/Justice* (New York: Columbia University Press, 1988), 36.

6. I am indebted to Andrew Koppelman and Stephen Macedo for helpful discussions on this point. See Andrew Koppelman's argument in chapter 4 of this volume, and Stephen Macedo's article "Homosexuality and the Conservative Mind," *Georgetown Law Journal* 84, no. 2 (1995), 261, 276.

7. For a fuller explication of this type of natural law argument, see John Finnis, "Law, Morality, and 'Sexual Orientation,'" *Notre Dame Law Review* 69, no. 5 (1994), 1049–76; revised, shortened, and reprinted in chapter 3 of this volume. For a cogent and well-developed response, see chapter 4, and Stephen Macedo, "Homosexuality and the Conservative Mind," *Georgetown Law Journal* 84, no. 2 (1995), 261–300.

8. The Ramsey Colloquium, "Homosexual Movement," 19.

9. Thomas Schmidt, "The Price of Love" in *Straight and Narrow? Compassion and Clarity in the Homosexuality Debate* (Downers Grove, IL: InterVarsity Press, 1995), chap. 6.

10. Both the American Psychological Association and the American Public Health Association have conceded this point: "Reliable data on the incidence of homosexual orientation are difficult to obtain due to the criminal penalties and social stigma attached to homosexual behavior and the consequent difficulty of obtaining representative samples of people to study" (*Amici Curiae* Brief in *Bowers v. Hardwick*, Supreme Court No. 85–140 [October Term 1985]).

11. It is worth noting that allegations of promiscuity are probably exaggerated. The study most commonly cited to prove homosexual male promiscuity, the Bell and Weinberg study, took place in 1978, in an urban center (San Francisco), at the height of the sexual revolution—hardly a broad sample. See Alan P. Bell and Martin S. Weinberg, *Homosexualities* (New York: Simon & Schuster, 1978). The far more recent and extensive University of Chicago study agreed that homosexual and bisexual people "have higher average numbers of partners than the rest of the sexually active people in the study," but it concluded that the differences in the mean number of partners "do not appear very large." See Edward O. Laumann et al., *The Social Organization of Sexuality: Sexual Practices in the United States* (Chicago: University of Chicago Press, 1994), 314, 316. I am grateful to Andrew Koppelman for drawing my attention to the Chicago study.

12. The Ramsey Colloquium, "Homosexual Movement," 19.

13. See S. R. Johnson, E. M. Smith, and S. M. Guenther, "Comparison of Gynecological Health Care Problems between Lesbian and Bisexual Women," *Journal of Reproductive Medicine* 32 (1987), 805–811.

14. See, for example, Stanton L. Jones, "The Loving Opposition," *Christianity Today* 37 no. 8 (July 19, 1993).

15. See Danya Glaser and Stephen Frosh, *Child Sexual Abuse*, 2nd ed. (Houndmills, England: Macmillan, 1993), 13–17; and Kathleen Coulbourn Faller, *Understanding Child Sexual Maltreatment* (Newbury Park, CA: Sage, 1990), 16–20.

16. See Frank G. Bolton Jr., Larry A. Morris, and Ann E. MacEachron, *Males at Risk: The Other Side of Child Abuse* (Newbury Park, CA: Sage, 1989), 61.

17. Part of the problem here arises from the grossly simplistic categorization of people into two (or, at best, three) sexual orientations; heterosexual, homosexual, and bisexual. Clearly, there is great variety within (and beyond) these categories. See Frederick Suppe, "Explaining Homosexuality: Philosophical Issues, and Who Cares Anyhow?" in Timothy F. Murphy, ed., *Gay Ethics: Controversies in Outing, Civil Rights, and Sexual Science* (New York: Harrington Park Press, 1994), esp. 223-268, published simultaneously in the Journal of Homosexuality 27, nos. 3–4: 223–268.

18. "An Essay on 'Paederasty'" in Robert Baker and Frederick Elliston, eds., *The Philosophy of Sex* (Buffalo, NY: Prometheus, 1984), 360–361. Bentham uses the word "paederast" where we would

use the term "homosexual"; the latter term was not coined until 1869, and the term "heterosexual" was coined a few years after that. Today, "pederasty" refers to sex between men and boys—a different phenomenon from the one Bentham was addressing.

19. The Ramsey Colloquium, "Homosexual Movement," 17–18.

20. The argument is a classic example of the fallacy of denying the antecedent: if *X* promotes procreation, then *X* is good; *X* does not promote procreation, therefore *X* is not good. Compare: if *X* is president, then *X* lives in the White House; Chelsea Clinton is not president, therefore Chelsea Clinton does not live in the White House.

21. Actually, Williams makes the point with regard to celibacy, while making an analogy between celibacy and homosexuality. See chapter 6 of this volume.

22. All biblical quotations are from the New Revised Standard Version.

23. See also Deut. 23:19, Lev. 25:35–37, Neh. 5:7–10, Jer. 15:10. Ezek. 22:12, and Luke 6:35. For a fuller explication of the analogy between homosexuality and usury, see John Corvino, "The Bible Condemned Usurers, Too," *Harvard Gay and Lesbian Review* 3, no. 4 (Fall 1996): 11–12.

24. See Richard P. McBrien, *Catholicism*, study ed. (San Francisco: Harper & Row, 1981). 1020.

25. *Loving v. Virginia*, 388 U.S. 1967.

26. One might object here that I am equivocating on the term "relationship," since throughout the paper I have been discussing acts, not relationships. But I maintain that Tommy and Jim's sexual act is *relational* in a way that Tommy and Fido's simply could not be. Even apart from their love for each other, Tommy and Jim have capacities for mutual communication and respect that Tommy and Fido simply do not have. Thus, one can approve of Tommy and Jim's sexual act without implying anything about Tommy and Fido's (possible) sexual acts: the two are fundamentally different.

Exercises

1. Write a three-page rebuttal to this essay, using real evidence and information you have researched. Be sure to address any plausible objections that could be directed at your argument.

2. Write a three-page assessment of the essay's argument. Consider each premise and the strength or validity of the reasoning. Take into account possible objections to your view.

3. Select a premise from Corvino's essay and evaluate it for plausibility. Do online research if you need to. Write a one-page summary of your evaluation.

Essay 5
More Innocents Die When
We Don't Have Capital Punishment

Dennis Prager

A couple of weeks ago, three New Hampshire prisoners, one a convicted murderer, escaped from prison. What if the murderer had murdered again? On whose hands would the victim's blood have been?

One of the most common, and surely the most persuasive, arguments against capital punishment is that the state may execute an innocent person. One reason for its effectiveness is that proponents of capital punishment often do not know how to respond to it.

That's a shame. For while the argument is emotionally compelling, it is morally and intellectually shallow.

First of all, there is almost no major social good that does not lead to the death of innocent individuals. Over a million innocent people have been killed and maimed in car accidents. Would this argue for the banning of automobiles? To those whose criterion for acceptable social policy is that not one innocent die, it should.

If it were proven that a strictly enforced 40-mile-per-hour speed limit on our nation's highways would save innocent lives, should we reduce highway limits to 40 miles per hour? Should all roller coasters be shut down because some, innocents get killed riding on them?

Anyone whose criterion for abolishing capital punishment is saving innocent lives should be for a 40-mile-per-hour speed limit and for abolishing roller coasters.

But death-penalty abolitionists aren't. And that is why they cannot logically build their case against capital punishment on the argument that an innocent may die. They accept a large number of social policies that kill innocents. Therefore, if abolitionists were intellectually honest, they would have to argue that capital punishment achieves no social good or that it is immoral to kill any murderers, not that it must be abandoned because an innocent may die.

But they do not make those arguments because they know that most Americans do not share their view that killing a murderer is immoral and that all murderers deserve to live. So they make the emotional but intellectually dishonest argument that, sure, some murderers ought be put to death, but we just can't do that because an innocent person may one day die.

The abolitionist argument that an innocent might be killed is false for a second reason. Far more innocent people have already died because we did not execute their murderers. The abolitionist has convinced himself, and a sincere but gullible public, that only a policy of capital punishment threatens innocent lives, while abolition of capital punishment threatens no innocent lives. That is entirely untrue.

Murderers who are not executed have murdered innocent people—usually fellow prisoners. And the very real possibility of escape from prison means that murderers threaten far more innocent lives than capital punishment does.

So here is the bottom line: If the escaped New Hampshire murderer had murdered someone, would opponents of capital punishment have acknowledged that the blood of that victim was on their hands? I doubt it. They believe that only advocates of capital punishment can have blood on their hands, when and if the state executes an innocent person. But they, the abolitionists, somehow have no blood on their hands when a convicted murderer murders an innocent.

As a proponent of capital punishment, I fully acknowledge my moral responsibility for any innocent person executed by the state. It is time that the abolitionists confronted their responsibility for every innocent already murdered and yet to be murdered by murderers who should have been executed. Or at least let them drop this false argument and state the truth: They believe murderers should never be killed.

Exercises

1. Outline the argument in this essay, indicating the premises and the conclusion. Determine whether the argument is deductive or inductive. Address the question of whether the argument is sound or cogent.

2. Write a two-page rebuttal to Essay 5. Spend at least a half hour online researching the topic.

3. Write a one-page essay defending Prager's argument. Then write another one-page essay arguing against his conclusion.

Essay 6
What's Wrong with Adultery?

Bonnie Steinbock

According to a 1980 survey in *Cosmopolitan*, 54 percent of American wives have had extramarital affairs; a study of 100,000 married women by the considerably tamer *Redbook* magazine found that 40 percent of the wives over 40 had been unfaithful. While such surveys are, to some extent, self-selecting—those who do it are more likely to fill out questionnaires about it—sexual mores have clearly changed in recent years. Linda Wolfe, who reported the results of the *Cosmopolitan* survey, suggests that "this increase in infidelity among married women represents not so much a deviation from traditional standards of fidelity as a break with the old double standard." Studies show that men have always strayed in significant numbers.

Yet 80 percent of "COSMO girls" did not approve of infidelity and wished their own husbands and lovers would be faithful. Eighty-eight percent of respondents to a poll taken in Iowa in 1983 viewed "coveting your neighbor's spouse" as a "major sin." It seems that while almost nobody approves of adultery, men have always done it, and women are catching up.

The increase in female adultery doubtless has to do with recent and radical changes in our attitudes toward sex and sexuality. We no longer feel guilty about enjoying sex; indeed, the capacity for sexual enjoyment is often regarded as a criterion of mental health. When sex itself is no longer intrinsically shameful, restraints on sexual behavior are loosened. In fact, we might question whether the abiding disapproval of infidelity merely gives lip service to an ancient taboo. Is there a rational justification for disapproving of adultery which will carry force with everyone, religious and nonreligious alike?

Trust and Deception

Note first that adultery, unlike murder, theft, and lying, is not universally forbidden. Traditional Eskimo culture, for example, regarded sharing one's wife with a visitor as a matter of courtesy. The difference can be explained by looking at the effects of these practices on social cohesiveness. Without rules protecting the lives, persons, and property of its members, no group could long endure.

Indeed, rules against killing, assault, lying, and stealing seem fundamental to having a morality at all.

Not so with adultery. For adultery is a private matter, essentially concerning only the relationship between husband and wife. It is not essential to morality like these other prohibitions: there are stable societies with genuine moral codes which tolerate extra-marital sex. Although adultery remains a criminal offense in some jurisdictions, it is rarely prosecuted. Surely this is because it is widely regarded as a private matter: in the words of Billie Holiday, "Ain't nobody's business if I do."

However, even if adultery is a private matter, with which the state should not interfere, it is not a morally neutral issue. Our view of adultery is connected to our thoughts and feelings about love and marriage, sex and the family, the value of fidelity, sexual jealousy, and exclusivity. How we think about adultery will affect the quality of our relationships, the way we raise our children, the kind of society we have and want to have. So it is important to consider whether our attitudes toward adultery are justifiable.

Several practical considerations militate against adultery: pregnancy and genital herpes immediately spring to mind. However, unwanted pregnancies are a risk of all sexual intercourse, within or without marriage; venereal disease is a risk of all non-exclusive sex, not just adulterous sex. So these risks do not provide a reason for objecting specifically to adultery. In any event, they offer merely pragmatic, as opposed to moral, objections. If adultery is wrong, it does not become less so because one has been sterilized or inoculated against venereal disease.

Two main reasons support regarding adultery as seriously immoral. One is that adultery is an instance of promise-breaking, on the view that marriage involves, explicitly or implicitly, a promise of sexual fidelity: to forsake all others. That there is this attitude in our culture is clear. Mick Jagger, not noted for sexual puritanism, allegedly refused to marry Jerry Hall, the mother of his baby, because he had no intension of accepting an exclusive sexual relationship. While Jagger's willingness to become an unwed father is hardly mainstream morality, his refusal to marry, knowing that he did not wish to be faithful, respects the idea that *marriage* requires such a commitment. Moreover, the promise of sexual fidelity is regarded as a very serious and important one. To cheat on one's spouse indicates a lack of concern, a willingness to cause pain, and so a lack of love. Finally, one who breaks promises cannot be trusted. And trust is essential to the intimate partnership of marriage, which may be irreparably weakened by its betrayal.

The second reason for regarding adultery as immoral is that it involves deception, for example, lying about one's whereabouts and relations with others. Perhaps a marriage can withstand the occasional lie, but a pattern of lying will have irrevocable consequences for a marriage, if discovered, and probably even if not. Like breaking promises, lying is regarded as a fundamental kind of wrong-doing, a failure to take the one lied to seriously as a moral person entitled to respect.

Open Marriage

These two arguments suffice to make most cases of adultery wrong, given the attitudes and expectations of most people. But what if marriage did not involve any promise of sexual fidelity? What if there were no need for deception, because neither partner expected or wanted such fidelity? Objections to "open marriage" cannot focus on promise-breaking and deception, for the expectation of exclusivity is absent. If an open marriage has been freely chosen by both spouses, and not imposed by a dominant on a dependent partner, would such an arrangement be morally acceptable, even desirable?

The attractiveness of extramarital affairs, without dishonesty, disloyalty, or guilt, should not be downplayed. However satisfying sex between married people may be, it cannot have the excitement of a new relationship. ("Not better," a friend once said defensively to his wife, attempting to explain his infidelity, "just *different*.") Might we not be better off, our lives fuller and richer, if we allowed ourselves the thrill of new and different sexual encounters?

Perhaps the expectation of sexual exclusivity in marriage stems from emotions which are not admirable: jealousy and possessiveness. That most people experience these feelings is no reason for applauding or institutionalizing them. Independence in marriage is now generally regarded as a good thing: too much "togetherness" is boring and stifling. In a good marriage, the partners can enjoy different activities, travel apart, and have separate friends. Why draw the line at sexual activity?

The natural response to this question invokes a certain conception of love and sex: sex is an expression of affection and intimacy and so should be reserved for people who love each other. Further, it is assumed that one can and should have such feelings for only one other person at any time. To make love with someone else is to express feelings of affection and intimacy that should be reserved for one's spouse alone.

This rejection of adultery assumes the validity of a particular conception of love and sex, which can be attacked in two ways. We might divorce sex from love and regard sex as a pleasurable activity in its own right, comparable to the enjoyment of a good meal. In his article "Is Adultery Immoral?"[1] Richard Wasserstrom suggests that the linkage of sex with love reflects a belief that unless it is purified by a higher emotion, such as love, sex is intrinsically bad or dirty.

But this is an overly simplistic view of the connection between sex and love. Feelings of love occur between people enjoying sexual intercourse, not out of a sense that sexual pleasure must be purified, but precisely because of the mutual pleasure they give one another. People naturally have feelings of affection for those who make them happy, and sex is a very good way of making someone extraordinarily happy. At the same time, sex is by its nature intimate, involving both physical and psychological exposure. This both requires and creates trust, which is closely allied to feelings of affection and love. This is not to say that sex necessarily requires or leads to love; but a conception of the relation between love and sex that ignores these factors is inadequate and superficial.

Alternatively, one might acknowledge the connection between sex and love, but attack the assumption of exclusivity. If parents can love all their children equally and if adults can have numerous close friends, why should it be impossible to love more than one sexual partner at a time? Perhaps we could learn to love more than one sexual partner at a time? Perhaps we could learn to love more widely and to accept that a spouse's sexual involvement with another is not a sign of rejection or lack of love.

The logistics of multiple involvement are certainly daunting. Having an affair (as opposed to a roll in the hay) requires time and concentration; it will almost inevitably mean neglecting one's spouse, one's children, one's work. More important, however, exclusivity seems to be an intrinsic part of "true love." Imagine Romeo pouring out his heart to both Juliet *and* Rosalind! In our ideal of romantic love, one chooses to forgo pleasure with other partners in order to have a unique relationship with one's beloved. Such "renunciation" is natural in the first throes of romantic love; it is precisely because this stage does not last that we must promise to be faithful through the notoriously unromantic realities of married life.

Fidelity as an Ideal

On the view I have been defending, genuinely open marriages are not *immoral*, although they deviate from a valued ideal of what marriage should be. While this is not the only ideal, or incumbent on all rational agents, it is a moral view in that it embodies a claim about a good way for people to live. The prohibition of adultery, then, is neither arbitrary nor irrational. However, even if we are justified in accepting the ideal of fidelity, we know that people do not always live up to the ideals they accept and we recognize that some failures to do so are worse than others. We regard a brief affair, occasioned by a prolonged separation, as morally different from installing a mistress.

Further, sexual activity is not necessary for deviation from the ideal of marriage which lies behind the demand for fidelity. As John Heckler observed during his bitter and public divorce from former Health and Human Services Secretary Margaret Heckler, "In marriage, there are two partners. When one person starts contributing far less than the other person to the marriage, that's the original infidelity. You don't need any third party." While this statement was probably a justification of his own infidelities, the point is valid. To abandon one's spouse, whether to a career or to another person, is also a kind of betrayal.

If a man becomes deeply involved emotionally with another woman, it may be little comfort that he is able to assure his wife that "Nothing happened." Sexual infidelity has significance as a sign of a deeper betrayal—falling in love with someone else. It may be objected that we cannot control the way we feel, only the way we behave; that we should not be blamed for falling in love, but only for acting on the feeling. While we may not have direct control over our feelings, however, we are responsible for getting ourselves into situations in which certain feelings naturally arise. "It just happened," is rarely an accurate portrayal of an extra-marital love affair.

If there can be betrayal without sex, can there be sex without betrayal? In the novel *Forfeit*, by Dick Francis, the hero is deeply in love with his wife, who was paralyzed by polio in the early days of their marriage. Her great unspoken fear is that he will leave her; instead, he tends to her devotedly. For several years, he forgoes sex, but eventually succumbs to an affair. While his adultery is hardly praiseworthy, it is understandable. He could divorce his wife and marry again, but it is precisely his refusal to abandon her, his continuing love and tender care, that makes us admire him.

People do fall in love with others and out of love with their spouses. Ought they refrain from making love while still legally tied? I cannot see much, if any, moral value in remaining physically faithful, on principle, to a spouse one no longer loves. This will displease those who regard the wrongness of adultery as a moral absolute, but my account has nothing to do with absolutes and everything to do with what it means to love someone deeply and completely. It is the value of that sort of relationship that makes sexual fidelity an ideal worth the sacrifice.

Neither a mere religiously based taboo, nor a relic of a repressive view of sexuality, the prohibition against adultery expresses a particular conception of married love. It is one we can honor in our own lives and bequeath to our children with confidence in its value as a coherent and rational ideal.

Note

1. In Wasserstrom's *Today's Moral Problems* (New York: Macmillan, 1975), 288–300. Reprinted in R. Baker and F. Elliston, eds., *Philosophy and Sex*, 1st ed. (Buffalo, NY: Prometheus, 1975), 207–21; 2nd ed. (1984), 93–106.

Exercises

1. Write a one-page summary of Steinbock's essay, noting what you consider its weakest premise and why you think that.

2. Write a three-page essay assessing Steinbock's argument, noting the truth or falsity of the premises and the strength or validity of the reasoning. Spend at least a half hour online researching the issue.

3. Write a three-page rebuttal to Steinbock. Consider possible objections to your view.

Essay 7
A Pat-Down Is Better than a Blow-Up

Caroline Baum

Imagine my horror when I read that two male Transportation Security Administration agents had singled out Orlando passenger Eliana Sutherland for further airport screening because of the size of her breasts.

As a woman, I was offended, outraged, disgusted—not to mention jealous. What does Eliana have that I don't have? No TSA agent has ever singled me out because of the size and shape of my breasts or any other body part.

All the outrage about full body scans and pat-downs seems off the point. What's the alternative? Yes, we could do it smarter (TSA, please contact Israel's Shin Bet immediately). Absent that, the latest techniques beat getting blown up in an airplane at 30,000 feet.

The objection to a full body scan from a vocal 15 percent of the populace, according to a CBS Poll, seems lame. It's hard to imagine the grainy images—about as racy as an X-ray—arousing anyone when far more graphic material is available at newsstands in most airports.

The TSA employs 56,000 people and has a budget of $8.2 billion, with $5.5 billion going toward airport security and screening. Airlines take security precautions as well. How many potential terrorists have been snagged by asking travelers, "Did you pack your own bags?" If you answered zero, you would be correct. What about, "Has anyone asked you to carry anything aboard this aircraft?" (Yes, and that ticking sound is driving me nuts!) One wonders what these employees would do if the passenger answered "no" in the first instance and "yes" in the second. Probably ask a supervisor.

In the same way the United States enacts new regulations to make sure the last financial crisis doesn't happen again, it excels at preventing a recurrence of the last terrorist attack. We haven't had another shoe bomber since Richard Reid attempted to blow up a plane in 2002 because we dutifully remove our shoes before going through security. But the TSA couldn't quite bring itself to institute strip searches after Umar Farouk Abdulmutallab tried to light up the skies last Christmas with a pair of explosive-packed Jockey shorts.

Could we do smarter security? Of course. We could learn a few things from the Israelis, maybe even outsource airport security to the Shin Bet, Israel's domestic security agency, which is charged with protecting El Al, the national airline. Ben-Gurion International Airport outside Tel Aviv has been recognized as the safest in the world. By the time passengers arrive at the airport, Israeli security agents know who they're looking for. The screening process begins when a ticket is booked.

Israel employs ethnic profiling, spending more time interviewing a young Arab male with a one-way ticket paid for in cash than an elderly Jewish grandmother or Hebrew University students off on a summer holiday. Muslim Arabs may be singled out unfairly, but they're the ones committed to the destruction of the Jewish state. It's this same group—albeit a small minority—that's targeting the United States.

Another thing: Israeli security agents are highly trained military veterans. They aren't looking for box cutters, toe nail scissors or liquid explosives. Israel's strategy is to "find the bomber, not the bomb," as the saying goes. Practical necessity trumps political correctness. El Al has at least one plainclothes armed marshal on all its flights. In 30 years it can boast a perfect record of no hijackings or hijacking attempts.

Israel has clearly figured out what works in a small nation surrounded by enemies. With two airports and 50 flights a day, it's easier to manage than our 450 airports and thousands of daily flights. Still I'm sure we would benefit from our Middle East ally's experience under fire.

Exercises

1. Write both an outline and a summary of this essay. Include the premises as well as the evidence or reasoning that supports them.

2. In a two-page essay, write an assessment of Baum's argument. Be explicit about whether you think the argument is good or bad and why.

3. Write a two-page rebuttal to Baum. That is, argue that pat-downs and other security measures are morally impermissible or impractical. Be sure to address any plausible objections that could be directed at your argument.

Essay 8
The Cohabitation Epidemic

Neil Clark Warren

A few summers ago, tennis stars Andre Agassi and Steffi Graf announced that their first child would be born. "This is a very exciting time for us," Agassi said. "We are so happy to be blessed with this gift." No one seemed to notice—or care—that the couple wasn't married. Only a generation ago, this revelation would have raised eyebrows.

Yes, things have changed dramatically over the past few decades. According to the U.S. Census Bureau, 1 million people were in "unmarried-partner households" in 1970. The number rose to 3.2 million in 1990. And in 2000, the figure soared to 11 million. Now, half of all Americans ages 35 to 39 have lived with someone outside of marriage, according to researcher Larry Bumpass. Make no mistake: We are witnessing a major societal shift before our very eyes.

When an epidemic reaches this level of societal acceptance, many well-meaning people begin to ask, "Should we accept cohabitation as another social trend akin to fast food, cell phones and casual Fridays?" You may be wondering whether all this hubbub about living together is much ado about nothing. As a psychologist who has worked with singles and married couples for 35 years, I think our alarm over this issue is much ado about a lot.

Who Cohabits and Why

Typically, people who cohabit fall into two categories. First, there are those who have little or no intention of getting married. They simply want to enjoy the benefits of living together—the availability of sex, combined financial resources, shared household responsibilities and so on. This arrangement allows for a "quick exit" if things turn sour. The second group are those who see living together as a trial marriage—a half-step toward the altar. These people say, "We'll live together first and see how it goes." They consider it prudent to take a test drive before signing on the dotted line.

Though I don't want to oversimplify a complex issue, I believe there are three primary reasons why these couples forgo or delay marriage:

1. Marriage has lost a lot of its luster in our society. The truth is, many people have never seen a successful, thriving marriage, mainly because great marriages are becoming scarce. Several years ago, I conducted a survey in which I asked 500 individuals to tell me about the marriage they most admired. To my dismay, nearly half said they couldn't recommend even one healthy, exemplary marriage! With such a dearth of model marriages, it's understandable why so many young people hesitate to take the plunge.

2. Beyond the lack of model marriages, millions of people have suffered significant pain from broken marriages. One researcher estimates that 70 percent of all Americans have been impacted by divorce—either their parents' or their own. When a broken marriage devastates someone's life, she or he may figure that getting married is just too risky.

3. The majority of singles have lost confidence in their ability to correctly judge a highly compatible and thus long-lasting match. Yet their needs for companionship, sexual satisfaction and economic sufficiency motivate them to search for a person with whom they can have at least a temporary partnership.

So Why Bother with Marriage?

We can certainly argue against cohabiting from a biblical standpoint, because numerous Scriptures admonish us to avoid sexual immorality and to keep marriage sacred (Hebrews 13:4, 1 Corinthians 6:18, 1 Thessalonians 4:3). But let's be realistic: Many couples who live together don't care about biblical principles, and even faith-oriented people often ignore what the Bible says. This is why psychological and other social science research becomes so critical. The findings of this research overwhelmingly support marriage over cohabitation. Consider:

Marriage vows serve as glue that holds people together. Numerous empirical studies destroy the myth that living together is good preparation for marriage, thus reducing the risk of divorce. In fact, one study involving 3,300 cases found that people who cohabited prior to marriage had a 46 percent higher marital failure rate than noncohabiters.

Think about it. The fundamental agreement upon which live-in relationships are based is conditional commitment. This attitude says, "I'll stick with you as long as things go well. But if we run into problems, all bets are off." Relationships that begin with a quasi-commitment carry the same mind-set into marriage. When things become trying, as inevitably they will from time to time, the spouses say goodbye.

As David Popenoe and Barbara Dafoe Whitehead wrote in their extensive review of recent literature, "Virtually all research on the subject has determined that the chances of divorce ending a marriage preceded by cohabitation are significantly greater than for a marriage not preceded by cohabitation."

Marriage provides the most stability for children. Few live-in couples intend to have children, but it often happens. More than a quarter of unmarried mothers are cohabiting at the time of their children's birth. Further, two-thirds of children who end up in stepfamilies have parents who are cohabiting rather than married.

This means that each year thousands of children are born or moved into families where Mom and Dad's commitment to each other is tenuous or, at least, informal. These children, during their most vulnerable developmental stages, are deprived of the security that comes from knowing their parents have pledged themselves to each other for a lifetime. To make matters worse, 75 percent of all children born to cohabiting parents will experience their parents' separation before they reach age 16. Only about one-third of children born to married parents face a similar fate.

Marriage offers promised permanence. Most wedding vows still include the promise to "love, honor and cherish in sickness and in health, in plenty or in want, till death do us part." One reason this is so important: The best relationships require partners who are genuine and authentic—who can be their real selves. The promised permanence of marriage allows just that: "I'll stick with you even when I come to know the real you, with all your imperfections and shortcomings." But how can two individuals be authentic and genuine if they think their partner may bolt at the first sign of trouble? With the conditional commitment of live-in relationships, partners are left wondering, If I'm not who my partner wants me to be—if he sees my faults—will he pack his bags and leave?

Marriage creates healthier individuals. Scores of studies have shown that married people are better off emotionally, physically, financially and vocationally than unmarried partners. For example, annual rates of depression among cohabiting couples are more than three times what they are among married couples. And women in cohabiting relationships are significantly more likely than married women to suffer physical and sexual abuse.

Marriage partners are more likely to be faithful. Four times as much infidelity is reported among cohabiting men than among married men. Moreover, one married woman in a hundred reports having had an affair in the past year, compared to 8 percent of cohabiting women.

Amid the alarming statistics about cohabitation, we can confidently tell singles that a "trial marriage" is unnecessary. In addition to the research showing the detriments of living together, several studies have discovered—with 80 percent to 94 percent accuracy—the variables that predict which marriages will thrive and which will not. This means unmarried couples can know in advance if they have a better-than-average chance of succeeding in marriage. With this available information, hopefully the cohabitation trend will begin to cycle downward.

Exercises

1. Study this essay and identify the rhetorical use of any euphemisms or dysphemisms and write a one-page paper about it.

2. Write a two-page rebuttal to Essay 8, assessing its argument and pointing out as many fallacies as possible.

3. Make a list of the support (studies, expert testimony, authority, statistics, etc.) that Warren uses to support his argument. Then write a two-page essay examining how strong or weak this evidence is and how it could be stronger.

Essay 9
Not Being Vaccinated Is Not Acceptable

David Ropeik

What does society do when one person's behavior puts the greater community at risk? We make them stop. We pass laws, or impose economic rules or find some other way to discourage individual behaviors that threaten the greater common good. You don't get to drive drunk. You don't get to smoke in public places. You don't even get to leave your house if you catch some particularly infectious disease.

Then what should we do about people who decline vaccination for themselves or their children and put the public at risk by fueling the resurgence of nearly eradicated diseases? Isn't this the same thing: one person's perception of risk producing behaviors that put others at risk? Of course it is. Isn't it time for society to say we need to regulate the risk created by the fear of vaccines? Yes, it is.

The evidence is overwhelming that declining vaccination rates are contributing to outbreaks of disease.

Take just one example, measles. The World Health Organization reports outbreaks in countries where vaccination rates have gone down, including France (7,000 cases so far this year, more than in all of 2010), Belgium, Germany, Romania, Serbia, Spain, Macedonia and Turkey. There have already been 334 measles cases in England and Wales this year, compared with 33 all of last year. The U. S. has seen 118 cases as of mid-May, compared with 56 cases a year from 2001 to 2008.

Small numbers, you say? True, but consider their cost (beyond the suffering of the patients), as illustrated in this case published this year by the Oxford Journals. When a woman from Switzerland who had not been vaccinated for measles visited Tucson in 2008 and became symptomatic, she went to a local hospital for medical attention.

This initiated a chain of events that over the next three months led to at least 14 people, including seven kids, getting measles. Seven of the victims caught the disease while visiting health care facilities. Four people had to be hospitalized. The outbreak cost two local hospitals a total of nearly $800,000, and the state and local health departments tens of thousands more, to track down the cases, quarantine and treat the sick and notify the thousands of people who might have been exposed.

Fueling that outbreak? None of the victims had been vaccinated or had "unknown vaccination status," and remarkably, 25 percent of the workers in the health care facilities where the patients were treated had no immunity to measles (either they had not been vaccinated or the antibodies from an earlier vaccination could no longer be detected). One health care worker got the disease and gave it to two other people.

That's just one example of the growing threat to public health caused by people worried that vaccines will cause autism and other harms, despite overwhelming evidence to the contrary. In many places, particularly in affluent, liberal, educated communities (San Diego, Marin County, Boulder, Colo.), un-vaccinated people are catching diseases that vaccines can prevent, like measles, whooping cough and meningitis.

In 2010, as California suffered its worst whooping cough outbreak in more than 60 years (more than 9,000 cases, 10 infant deaths), Marin County had one of the lowest rates of vaccination statewide and the second-highest rate of whooping cough. A 2008 study in Michigan found that areas with "exemption clusters" of parents who didn't vaccinate their kids were three times more likely to have outbreaks of whooping cough than areas where vaccination rates matched the state average.

And this is a risk to far more people than just those who have opted out of vaccination. People are getting sick who have been vaccinated but the vaccine either doesn't work or has weakened. Infants too young to be vaccinated are getting sick, and some of them are dying horrible deaths from whooping cough after exposure in communities where "herd immunity" has fallen too low to keep the spread of the disease in check.

Unvaccinated people who get sick and visit doctor's offices or hospitals increase the danger for anyone else who uses those facilities.

Outbreaks are costing the health care system millions of dollars, and local and state government (that's taxpayer money, yours and mine) millions more as they try to chase down each outbreak and bring it under control to protect the public's health. Your health, and mine.

No one doubts the honest passion of those who fear vaccines. And for some people, no amount of communication or dialogue or reasoning will stop them from worrying. But risk perception is ultimately subjective, a combination of the facts and how those facts feel, and sometimes our fears don't match the evidence. The dangers that sometimes arise because of the way we perceive risk must be managed too. But we must act in the face of this threat to public health.

There are many potential solutions, each fraught with pros and cons and details that require careful thought and open democratic discussion.

- Perhaps it should be harder to opt out of vaccination. (Twenty-one states allow parents to decline vaccination of their children simply for "philosophical" reasons; 48 allow a religious exemption, but few demand documentation from parents to support claims that their faith precludes vaccination.)

- Perhaps there should be higher health care and insurance costs for unvaccinated people, or "healthy behavior" discounts for people who do get vaccinated, paid for from what society saves by avoiding the spread of disease.

- There could be restrictions on the community and social activities in which unvaccinated people can participate, like lengthy school trips for kids, etc.

This is not about creating more government to intrude further into our lives. This is about calling on government to do what it's there for in the first place: to protect us from the actions of others when as individuals we can't protect ourselves. It is appropriate, and urgent, that we act to protect public health from those whose choices about vaccines are putting the rest of us at risk: We make them stop.

Exercises

1. Write a three-page assessment of this essay's argument. Consider each premise and the strength or validity of the reasoning.

2. Write both an outline and a summary of this essay. Include the premises as well as the evidence or reasoning that supports them.

3. Go online to research the controversy over whether there is a strong link between autism and vaccinations. Then write a three-page essay arguing either for or against the theory. Be sure to address any plausible objections that could be directed at your argument.

Essay 10
Women and the Afghanistan Peace Process

Ann Jones

Looking for a way out of Afghanistan? Maybe it's time to try something totally different, like putting into action, for the first time in history, the most enlightened edict ever passed by the U. N. Security Council: Resolution 1325.

Passed on Oct. 31, 2000, the resolution was hailed worldwide as a great victory for both women and international peace. In a nutshell, it calls for women to participate equally in all processes of conflict resolution, peacemaking and reconstruction.

The resolution grew out of a recognition that while men at the negotiating table still jockey for power and wealth, women who are included commonly advocate for interests that coincide perfectly with those of civil society. They are concerned about their children and consequently about shelter, clean water, sanitation, jobs, health care, education—the things that make life livable for peaceable people.

It's been nine years since I started doing aid work in Afghanistan, and I am frustrated by the lack of progress toward a peaceful and livable society.

Yet whenever I present my modest proposal for the implementation of 1325 to American big men who lay claim to expertise on Afghanistan, most of them strongly object. They know the theory, they say, but they are precluded from throwing their weight behind the resolution by delicate considerations of "cultural relativism." Afghanistan, they remind me, is a "traditional" culture when it comes to women. Westerners, they say, must respect that.

Yet the eagerness of Western men to defer to this "tradition" seems excessive, especially since few of the Afghan men who actually governed Afghanistan between 1919 and 1989 would have shared their sentiments.

Modern ideas, including the idea of equality between the sexes, have been at the heart of Afghan cultural struggles for at least a century. In the 1920s, King Amanullah founded the first high school for girls and the first family court to adjudicate women's complaints about their husbands; he proclaimed the equality of men and women, banned polygamy and the burka and banished ultra-conservative mullahs who undermined the moderate Sufi ideals of Afghanistan. His modern ideas cost him his crown, but Amanullah and his modern, unveiled queen, Soraya, are remembered for their brave endeavor to drag the country into the modern world.

Thousands of Afghan citizens have shared Amanullah's modern views, expressed later by successive leaders, kings and communists alike. But in 2001 the United States—and by extension the entire international community—cast its lot with Hamid Karzai.

We put him in power after a power-sharing conference in Bonn, to which only two Afghan women were invited. We paid millions to stage two presidential elections, in 2004 and 2009, and looked the other way while Karzai's men stuffed the ballot boxes. Now, it seems, we're stuck with him and his ultraconservative, misogynist "traditions," even though an ever-growing number of Afghanistan watchers now identify the Karzai government as the single greatest problem the United States faces in its never-ending war.

And what has Karzai done for the women of Afghanistan? Not a thing.

That's the conclusion of a recent report issued by the Human Rights Research and Advocacy Consortium, an association of prominent aid and independent research groups in Afghanistan. Afghan researchers conducted extensive interviews with prominent male religious scholars, male political leaders and female leaders at the local, provincial and national levels.

The report notes that Karzai has supported increasingly repressive laws against women, most notoriously the "Taliban-style" Shia Personal Status Law, which not only legitimizes marital rape but prevents women from stepping out of their homes without their husbands' consent. The report points out that this law denies women even the basic freedoms guaranteed all citizens in Afghanistan's 2004 constitution.

In fact, Karzai's record on human rights, as the report documents, is chiefly remarkable for what he has not done. He holds extraordinary power to make political appointments, yet today, after nearly 10 years in office, only one Cabinet ministry is led by a woman: the Ministry for Women's Affairs, which has only advisory powers.

Karzai has appointed only one female provincial governor, Dr. Habiba Sarabi, among 33 men. (Is it by chance that her province, Bamiyan, is generally viewed as the most peaceful in the country?) Among Afghanistan's city governments, he has named only one female mayor. And to the Supreme Court High Council, he has appointed no women at all.

It should come as no surprise, then, that when Karzai named a High Peace Council to negotiate with the Taliban, its members initially consisted of 60 men and no women. They were the usual suspects: warlords, Wahhabis, mujahedin, all fighting for power to the bitter end. Under international pressure, Karzai belatedly added 10 women to the group. The United States has signed off on this lopsided "peace" council.

I suppose this means my modest proposal doesn't stand a chance, and that's a shame. We know from experience that power-sharing agreements among combatants tend to fray, often unraveling into open warfare within a few years. We also know that just because the big men in power stop shooting at each other doesn't mean they stop the war against civilians—especially women and girls. Rape, torture, mutilation and murder continue unabated or increase.

Thus, from the standpoint of civilians, a war is not always over when it's "over," and the "peace" is not necessarily a real peace at all. Think of the Democratic Republic of Congo, the notorious rape capital of the world, where thousands upon thousands of women have been gang-raped even though the country has been officially at peace since 2003.

I don't expect men in power to take seriously the Security Council's proposition that the involvement of women in negotiations makes for a better and more lasting peace.

Progressive, peaceable men would prefer to live in a peace created by women and men together. But too many big men, in both Afghanistan and the United States, are doing very nicely, thank you, with the traditional arrangements in their country and ours.

Exercises

1. Write an outline and a one-half page summary of this essay.

2. In a two-page essay state whether you agree with Jones and give reasons for your view. Consider possible objections to your view.

3. Go online to research women's rights in Afghanistan or Saudi Arabia. Then write a three-page essay explaining how women's rights are restricted and why women should have the same rights as men.

Essay 11
A Deviance from God's Norm

Richard Land

Recently, Senator Rick Santorum was attacked by the liberal media, politicians, and pro-homosexual groups for comments he made about a case being argued currently before the U.S. Supreme Court.

The plaintiff in this case, who was arrested by Houston sheriff's deputies and fined for engaging in homosexual behavior outlawed in Texas, is attempting to have Texas' anti-sodomy law ruled unconstitutional. When asked by an Associated Press reporter to state his opinion about homosexual behavior, Mr. Santorum referred to the Supreme Court case and commented that activities like sodomy "undermine the basic tenets of our society and the family."

In return for stating his honest opinion Mr. Santorum has been subjected to an endless, venomous diatribe. Liberals and pro-homosexual groups have decided that Mr. Santorum is bigoted and intolerant and no longer worthy material for Senate leadership. The treatment Mr. Santorum has endured for stating his opinion—which by the way, is the opinion of the vast majority of Americans— serves as a vivid reminder of the tactics of his attackers.

Because the homosexual-rights groups have been unable to persuade the majority of Americans that homosexuality is good for us, they have resorted to attacking anyone who speaks the majority opinion. In so doing the gay thought police have revealed themselves for what they really are—bullies who threaten and intimidate those who dare to speak out against them.

We must ask who the real bigots are here. In America, speaking one's mind is a Constitutionally-protected right. The real bigots are those who label anyone who disagrees with them as bigoted and intolerant and attack them for sharing their beliefs. Mr. Santorum has not called for anyone's resignation or dismissal. His detractors have. Once again, the homosexual-rights groups have revealed that they are the real bigots.

Our society has the responsibility and the right to discourage the practice of homosexuality. The Judeo-Christian teaching on this is clear. Homosexuality is a deviance from God's norm. It is neither normal nor healthy behavior. Lest anyone think that this theological position is merely sectarian, it is important to note that even the renowned theologian Wolfhart Pannenberg concluded that when the church has "ceased to treat homosexual activity as a departure from the biblical norm" it "would no longer stand on biblical ground but against the unequivocal witness of Scripture" and "would thereby have ceased to be one, holy, catholic, and apostolic."

Furthermore, any attempt to equate homosexuality with race or ethnicity should offend all of us. There is no evidence that homosexuality is an inborn trait, in spite of numerous efforts to prove the contrary. Homosexuality has many contributing causes, but it is obviously not to be equated with race or ethnicity. A person's ethnicity is what one is, whereas homosexual behavior is what one does.

As Christians, we will continue to support politicians who speak out against homosexuality and to oppose those who support special rights for homosexuals and who seek to support

societal approval of homosexual behavior. I applaud Mr. Santorum for courageously sharing his beliefs. We hope other politicians will be emboldened by his stand to hold firm to
their convictions about the immorality of homosexual behavior and resist the bullying and
intimidation tactics of radical homosexual-rights groups.

Exercises

1. Write both an outline and a summary of this essay. Include the premises as well as the evidence or reasoning that support them.

2. In a three-page paper, compare Land's argument with that in Essay 4. Decide which essay makes the stronger case and explain your reasons for thinking so.

3. Identify the premises and conclusions of any arguments in this essay and write a two-page rebuttal. As part of your critique, identify any fallacies used by the author.

Essay 12
Marriage Still Evolving, as Ever

Buffalo News

April 2, 2006

The refrain echoes from pulpit to parishioner, from megaphone to protester, from blogger to reader: Marriage is a bond between a man and a woman, and *only* that.

In most cases, perhaps 90 percent, it is. But as New York prepares for a Court of Appeals decision this summer that could legalize or pave the way for gay marriage, people might want to try getting their heads around the idea that marriage is and has been many things. But it never was engraved in romantic, heterosexual—even monogamous—marble. Marriage is an evolving, dynamic, living arrangement.

Marriage only recently, say in the last 150 years, focused on two people in love. Before that, it was more often than not—at all income levels—a forced or coerced arrangement about status, property or power. You could be a prince or a pauper, but your father was often trying to enhance his kingdom., or diet, by hooking you up with someone who could help him do that.

There was a time when women entering marriage lost all their rights to their husbands, something most women today would find laughable. Even more extreme, women at one time, as part of marriage, became a man's property. There were laws in this country that said marriage protected men against accusations of spousal rape. If you were a woman, your husband could rape you with impunity. Marriage, by law or custom, was restricted along racial or religious lines. "Intermarriage" was viewed as hurting or weakening a race, religion or group.

Finally, marriage used to be unviolable, something impossible to split. Today divorce is routine, with half ending before death do us part. That may or may not be good for society, children and spouses, but it shows how marriage is still evolving.

So when supporters talk about gays and lesbians marrying—and thereby gaining an estimated 1,500 rights that accrue to married people but are routinely denied to gays—it's more evolution. You may not agree; you may believe that *only* men and women should marry. But as more states approve, it might help to understand marriage's history and its dynamic place in our lives by examining its fluid reality.

Exercises

1. Write an outline and a one-half page summary of this essay.

2. Identify the conclusion and premises of the argument, and write a one-page rebuttal to it.

3. In a two-page paper compare this essay with Essay 8 ("The Cohabitation Epidemic") and determine which one makes the stronger argument and why.

Essay 13
Slouching toward Chimeras

Jeremy Rifkin

What happens when you cross a human and a mouse? Sounds like the beginning of a bad joke but, in fact, it's a serious high tech experiment recently carried out by a research team headed by a distinguished molecular biologist, Irving Weissman, at Stanford University's Institute of Cancer/Stem Cell Biology and Medicine. Scientists injected human brain cells into mouse fetuses, creating a strain of mice that were approximately 1 percent human. Dr. Weissman is actively considering a follow-up experiment that would produce mice whose brains are 100 percent human.

What if the mice escaped the laboratory and began to proliferate in the outside environment? What might be the ecological consequences of mice who think like human beings, let loose in nature? Dr. Weissman says he would keep a tight rein on the mice and if they showed any signs of humaneness he would kill them. Hardly reassuring.

In a world where the bizarre has become all too commonplace, few things any longer shock the human psyche. But, experiments like the one that produced a partially humanized mouse at Stanford University stretch the limits of human tinkering with nature to the realm of the pathological.

The new research field at the cutting edge of the biotech revolution is called chimeric experimentation. Researchers around the world are combining human and animal cells and creating chimeric creatures that are part human and part animal, reminiscent of the ancient Greek chimeric myths of human-animal hybrids.

The first such chimeric experiment occurred many years ago when scientists in Edinburgh, Scotland fused together a sheep and goat embryo—two completely unrelated animal species that are incapable of mating and producing a hybrid offspring in nature. The resulting creature, called a Geep, was born with the head of a goat and the body of a sheep.

Now, scientists have their sights trained on breaking the final taboo in the natural world—crossing humans and animals to create new human-animal hybrids of every kind and description. Already, aside from the humanized mouse, scientists have created pigs with human blood running through their veins and sheep with livers and hearts that are mostly human.

The experiments are designed to advance medical research. Indeed, a growing number of genetic engineers argue that human-animal hybrids will usher in a golden era of medicine. Researchers say that the more humanized they can make research animals, the better able they will be to model the progression of human diseases, test new drugs, and harvest tissues and organs for transplantation into human bodies. What they fail to mention is that there are other equally promising and less invasive alternatives to these kinds of bizarre experiments including sophisticated computer modeling to study diseases and test the effectiveness and toxicity of drugs as well as in vitro tissue culture, nanotechnology, and artificial prostheses to substitute for human tissue and organs. When it comes to chimeric experimentation, then, the question is, at what price?

Some researchers are speculating about human-chimpanzee chimeras—creating a humanzee. A humanzee would be the ideal laboratory research animal because chimpanzees are so closely related to human beings. Chimps share 98 percent of the human genome and a fully mature chimp has the equivalent mental abilities and consciousness of a four-year-old human child. Fusing a human and chimpanzee embryo—a feat researchers say is quite feasible—could produce a creature so human that questions regarding its moral and legal status would throw 4,000 years of human ethics into utter chaos.

Would such a creature enjoy human rights and protections under the law? For example, it's possible that such a creature could cross the species barrier and mate with a human. Would society allow inter-species conjugation? Would a humanzee have to pass some kind of "humanness" test to win its freedom? Would it be forced into doing menial labor or be used to perform dangerous activities?

The horrific possibilities are mind-boggling. For example, what if human stem cells—the primordial cells that turn into the body's 200 or so cell types—were to be injected into an animal embryo and spread throughout the animal's body into every organ? Some human cells could migrate to the testes and ovaries where they could grow into human sperm and eggs. If two of the chimeric mice were to mate, they could potentially conceive a human embryo. If the human embryo were to be removed and implanted in a human womb, the resulting human baby's biological parents would have been chimeric mice.

Please understand that none of this is science fiction. The American National Academy of Sciences, the country's most august scientific body, issued guidelines for chimeric research on April 25, anticipating a flurry of new experiments in the burgeoning field of human-animal chimeric experimentation. What would be the ramifications of creating hundreds, even thousands, of new life forms that are part human and part other creature? Creatures that could mate, reproduce, and repopulate the Earth?

Bio-ethicists are already clearing the moral path for human-animal chimeric experiments, arguing that once society gets past the revulsion factor, the prospect of new, partially human creatures has much to offer the human race. And, of course, this is exactly the kind of reasoning that has been put forth time and again to justify what is fast becoming a macabre journey into a monstrous Brave New World in which all of nature can be ruthlessly manipulated and reengineered to suit the momentary needs and even whims and caprices of just one species, the Homo sapiens. But now, with human-animal chimeric experiments, we risk even undermining our own species' biological integrity in the name of human progress.

With chimeric technology, scientists now have the power to rewrite the evolutionary saga—to sprinkle parts of the Homo sapiens species into the rest of the animal kingdom as well as fuse parts of other species into our own genome and even to create new human subspecies and superspecies. Are we on the cusp of a biological renaissance, as some believe, or sowing the seeds of our own destruction? Perhaps it is time to ask what we mean by progress.

Exercises

1. Study this essay, identify its conclusion and premises, and write a two-page rebuttal to it. Consider possible objections to your view.

2. Write a two-page assessment of this essay's argument. Consider each premise and the strength or validity of the reasoning.

3. In a half page identify this essay's weakest premise and explain how you would strengthen the argument.

Essay 14
Fighting Islamic Extremists Who Stifle Free Speech

Ayaan Hirsi Ali and Daniel Huff

Earlier this year, after Comedy Central altered an episode of *South Park* that had prompted threats because of the way it depicted Islam's prophet Muhammad, Seattle cartoonist Molly Norris proposed an "Everybody Draw Muhammad Day." The idea was, as she put it, to stand up for the First Amendment and "water down the pool of targets" for extremists.

The proposal got Norris targeted for assassination by radical Yemeni American cleric Anwar Awlaki, who has been linked to the attempted Christmas Day bombing of a Northwest Airlines flight and also to several of the 9/11 hijackers. This month, after warnings from the FBI, Norris went into hiding. The *Seattle Weekly* said that Norris was "moving, changing her name and essentially wiping away her identity."

It's time for free-speech advocates to take a page from the abortion rights movement's playbook. In the 1990s, abortion providers faced the same sort of intimidation tactics and did not succumb. Instead, they lobbied for a federal law making it a crime to threaten people exercising reproductive rights and permitting victims to sue for damages. The Freedom of Access to Clinic Entrances Act, or FACE, passed in 1994 by solid bipartisan margins. A similar act is needed to cover threats against free-speech rights.

A federal law would do two things. First, it would deter violent tactics, by focusing national attention on the problem and invoking the formidable enforcement apparatus of the federal government. Second, its civil damages provision would empower victims of intimidation to act as private attorneys general to defend their rights.

Such an act is overdue. Across media and geographies, Islamic extremists are increasingly using intimidation to stifle free expression.

In 2004, Theo van Gogh was murdered on an Amsterdam street in broad daylight for his film criticizing Islam's treatment of women. By 2006, it was reported that "dozens of people" across Europe were "in hiding or under police protection because of threats from Muslim extremists."

Some targets, including the co-author of this commentary, fled to the United States, where it seemed safer—and so it is, for now. However, the stark truth is that the United States was never immune and the situation is deteriorating.

In 1989, two American bookstores carrying Salman Rushdie's *The Satanic Verses* were firebombed. Spooked major chains took it off display. And there have been many more threats that received less publicity. Few have heard, for example, about Oklahoma atheist Sabri Husibi, who received death threats after writing a 2009 article critical of his former faith. His aged mother in Syria was warned she would never see him again. "Clearly shaken," he requested the paper that published his article clarify that he is critical of all faiths.

These kinds of threats have had a formidable chilling effect. Mindful of the retaliation others faced, Yale University Press, the Met, the director of the disaster epic *2012* and countless others have decided to pre-emptively censor themselves.

The kind of legislation we propose is essential if we are to win the war of ideas against extremists, who use threats to drive the moderate message out of public discourse.

Existing state laws prohibiting intimidation are inadequate. On the criminal side, the heightened standard of proof deters prosecutors from investing scarce resources. Explicit grounds for a civil action do not always exist, and damages can be difficult to quantify. By contrast, the FACE Act, which provides the model for the proposed legislation, lets victims opt for preset damages.

The *South Park* incident neatly illustrates the benefits. On April 15, following the first of a two-part episode mocking Jesus, Buddha and Muhammad, RevolutionMuslim.com announced that "(w)e have to warn Matt and Trey that what they are doing is stupid and they will probably wind up like Theo van Gogh." The "warning" included the names, photos and work address of the *South Park* creators, a graphic image of van Gogh's mutilated body and pictures of other targets of Muslim extremists. Overlaying this was audio of Awlaki preaching about assassinating anyone who defamed the prophet. Panicked, Comedy Central heavily censored the episode.

This rather obvious threat could not be prosecuted. New York Police Department officials explained it did not rise to a crime. Were the FACE Act applicable here, a civil suit would have been available, and precedent suggests it would have been successful.

In 2002, on very similar facts, the U.S. 9th Circuit Court of Appeals upheld a civil award to doctors who sued using the FACE Act. A fringe pro-life group, the American Coalition of Life Activists, had in various public venues displayed "Wanted"-style posters bearing the names, photos and addresses of doctors who performed abortions. Their names were also posted on the Internet alongside a list of wounded and murdered doctors whose names were struck through. The court held that the ACLA's activities constituted true threats unprotected by the First Amendment.

If we leave our artists, activists and thinkers alone to weather the assault, they will succumb and we will all suffer the consequences.

Exercises

1. Write a one-page summary of this essay, noting what you consider to be its weakest premise and why you think so.

2. Write a two-page essay assessing the argument, noting the truth or falsity of its premises, the strength or validity of the reasoning, and possible objections to the essay's thesis.

3. In a two-page paper, discuss one of the examples of extremist attacks on free speech given by Hirsi Ali and Huff, explain how such incidents affect free speech, and argue that they should not be tolerated by democratic governments.

Essay 15
Is Sluttishness a Feminist Statement?

Wendy Kaminer

Fifty years after the onset of the modern feminist movement, sexual violence remains a primary issue, especially for young women asserting their right to dress or undress as they choose. The "slut walk" is the latest protest gimmick, inspired by the stupidity of a Toronto police officer who advised women (rather unoriginally) to "avoid dressing like sluts in order not to be victimized." So, to make their point about victim blaming, women are proclaiming their sluttishness, trying to reframe it as a healthy, confident sexual choice; they're "reappropriating" the word *slut*, along with its dress code, while simultaneously protesting their sexual objectification.

Good luck with that. A more dissonant strategy is hard to imagine. You don't have to share the dim-witted belief that rape is caused even partly by provocatively dressed females to suspect that tottering around half-naked in stilettos may not be the most effective way for women to discourage their objectification.

I'm not making moral judgments about women's sartorial or sexual preferences; I sympathize with the desire to demoralize discussions of female sexuality. I'm simply questioning the utility of sluttishness in a fight against sexual violence. My concerns are practical, not moral; as a practical matter, we can control the way we present ourselves but not the ways in which we are perceived. Young women who proudly dress like sluts intending only to assert their sexual confidence should not be surprised if some onlookers believe that they're advertising their availability as sexual toys. They should expect at least occasionally to be evaluated by their forms and not their intellectual or characterological contents.

Indeed, celebrating sluttishness probably encourages girls to rely on appearances; it tends to reduce sexuality, and self-regard, to a matter of appearance. A recent study from Kenyon College considering the influence of girl's clothing styles on their "self-objectification" determined that about 25 percent of the clothes found in popular stores for girls was "sexualized." Of course, sexualized dress is a fairly subjective concept: the Kenyon researchers defined it as "clothing that revealed or emphasized a sexualized body part, had characteristics associated with sexiness, and/or had sexually suggestive writing." But talk to the mothers with young daughters, and you can accumulate a lot of anecdotal evidence and concern about the naïve idealization of sluttishness and the "power" it gives girls over boys. It's a perverse version of feminism that encourages sexually vulnerable girls to feel protected by highly sexualized femininity.

Slut walks seem about as likely to advance a feminist agenda as Disney princesses or the viewing parties organized around the wedding of Will and Kate. Princesses or sluts? Virgins or whores? The choices are familiar, like the belief that girls and women are empowered by aggressively asserting their sexuality, in the most conventional ways. Power sluttishness was the theme of *Cosmo* girls decades ago and was reinvented by lipstick feminism (and Madonna) in the 1990s. It has always held obvious, understandable appeal to young women eager to disassociate from the stereotypical image of feminists as unattractive, desexualized, and (at least aspirationally) emasculating.

But lipstick feminism, under various rubrics, has contributed to feminism's incoherence, effectively embracing or "appropriating" sexual objectification in the vain hope of defeating it and positing sexual allure as a political act. It is, however, a *personal* act, and the personal is often apolitical. Celebrating depoliticized female empowerment, lipstick feminism helped confer popular feminist credibility on such antifeminist celebrities as Sarah Palin. The feminist movement has never been monolithic; women's rights advocates have been divided historically by differing visions of equality or protectionism for women, individualism or collectivism, as well as by class and racial conflicts. But these days feminism is so splintered and so ideologically confused that it barely exists as a movement at all.

That's too bad for women, because they're regularly losing fundamental rights, most notably their rights to privacy and reproductive choice. At the state and federal levels, lawmakers have proposed or enacted a long list of prohibitive limitations on access to abortion; intrusive conditions on women seeking abortions (like mandatory sonograms); and financial burdens or punishments for women who obtain abortions and for organizations that provide them (notably Planned Parenthood, which is primarily devoted to women's health care). Meanwhile, not surprisingly, the right to dress like a slut remains secure.

Exercises

1. Write both an outline and a summary of this essay. Include the premises as well as the evidence or reasoning that supports them.

2. In a two-page paper, evaluate this essay's argument and explain whether you agree with its conclusion and why.

3. Write your own three-page essay on this topic, laying out your argument, supporting the premises, and defending your view against at least one objection.

Essay 16
Freedom of Expression: Protect Student Speech—Even "Unwise" Bong Banner

USA Today

March 21, 2007

The 18-year-old high school student in Juneau, Alaska, who unfurled a "BONG HiTS 4 JESUS" banner on a sidewalk across from his school when the Olympic torch passed by in 2002 says he was merely trying to provoke his school's strict principal and get himself on TV.

If that was the goal, he certainly succeeded. The principal did get angry. Concluding that "bong hits" clearly meant pot smoking, she crumpled up the banner, suspended the student for 10 days and touched off a free-speech dispute that's pending before the U.S. Supreme Court. The case sounds like something out of *Ferris Bueller's Day Off*, the 1986 film featuring a wisecracking senior who bedevils the dean of students. But the court's decision, likely to come by the end of June, is expected to be an important marker of the limits of student expression—one that should be settled in the student's favor.

As any principal knows, kids often say and do things adults find dumb and offensive; when that happens at school, it's reasonable to restrict disruptive speech that interferes with education. But the bong-banner incident neither took place on school property nor disrupted classroom activity.

Teachers and principals have to make tough calls like these every day, and their authority extends off campus to school-connected events such as field trips or football games. Yet the courts have appropriately set a high bar for limiting student speech: Their standard is a landmark 1969 Supreme Court ruling that allowed students to wear black arm bands to protest the Vietnam War, because students didn't give up their free speech rights "at the schoolhouse gate" unless their actions significantly disrupted or interfered with school activities. " In the Juneau case, the school board, joined by the Bush administration, is asking the court to lower that bar by redefining "disruption" to mean not just interfering with the educational environment, but also interfering with the school's "educational mission." They make a superficially appealing case. The principal found the bong banner obnoxious and embarrassing, particularly in light of the school's anti-drug policy, and she saw no reason not to discipline students for flouting that policy, even off school grounds.

But where to draw the line? How can the court best balance the principal's need to control her school against students' right to express their opinions, particularly political or religious opinions? Several religious groups filed briefs on the student's behalf.

When the case was argued Monday before the Supreme Court, the justices bantered about what other banners would or wouldn't be permissible: "Vote Republican"? "Smoke Pot, It's Fun"? "Rape is Fun"? "Extortion is Profitable"?

They reached no obvious conclusions, and there was no claim that "BONG HiTS 4 JESUS" was articulate, reasoned or much more than the nonsensical statement the student intended when he took a slogan he saw on a snowboard and turned it into a banner meant to anger an authority figure.

But the line around protected speech is appropriately wide, even when it's subversive or sophomoric. The student's attorney was on target when he told the justices that this sort of expression is "the kind of speech we must tolerate, no matter how unwise it is."

If students don't shed their free-speech rights at the schoolhouse gate, they surely don't on the public sidewalk across the street from the school.

Exercises

1. Write a three-page paper arguing against the claim defended in this essay. Be sure to address any plausible objections that could be directed at your argument.

2. Write a three-page essay in which you argue that student speech should not be protected.

3. Study this essay and Essay 17 ("Freedom of Expression: Policy Reflects Common Sense"). Decide which essay presents the stronger argument, and write a paper defending your view.

Essay 17
Freedom of Expression:
Policy Reflects Common Sense

Kenneth W. Starr

One year ago, the U.S. Court of Appeals for the 9th Circuit issued a decision that confounded school boards and administrators nationwide. A conscientious public high school principal enforced a longstanding student conduct policy against a student entrusted to her care. For that entirely appropriate action, the 9th Circuit subjected her to the prospect of punitive damages.

Principal Deborah Morse was in charge of a school event celebrating the Olympic Torch Relay as it arrived in Alaska for the first time ever. The event occurred during school hours. The assembled student body (accompanied by teachers and administrators) lined both sides of the street in front of the school. Cheerleaders were in uniform. The pep band played. And four students acted as torchbearers. At the very moment that the torch (and television cameras) arrived in front of the school, then-senior high school student Joseph Frederick unfurled his now-famous banner festooned with the slang marijuana reference, "BONG HiTS 4 JESUS."

Principal Morse reasonably determined on the spot that Frederick's obtrusive sign violated school policy prohibiting students from advocating the use of substances that are illegal to minors. This policy expressly applied to on- and off-campus activities. School rules such as this are commonplace throughout the country.

For decades, local school officials, acting in *loco parentis*, have relied on these policies to convey that illegal substances are wrong and harmful. In view of the staggering drug problem in America—half of high school students use drugs illegally by graduation, often on school property—policies that keep pro-drug messages out of the school environment reflect common sense.

Frederick certainly may have a First Amendment right to display his banner on his own time, out of school. But in stealing the focus of a school event for his own drug-promoting publicity stunt, he ran afoul of a reasonable regulation. It would be unwise for the Supreme Court to follow the 9th Circuit in rendering such rules unenforceable. The Court should not compound further the problem by allowing a lifelong educator like Deborah Morse to be saddled with the specter of a draconian civil damages lawsuit.

Exercises

1. Write a paper in rebuttal to this essay. Use an argument that is not put forward in Essay 16 ("Freedom of Expression: Protect Student Speech— Even 'Unwise' Bong Banner").

2. In a two-page paper, defend the proposition that free speech can be curtailed by the government only if the speech incites violence.

3. In a two-page paper, argue that free speech can never be curtailed just because it offends someone.